Marsden Samuel, Gary Staff

The German Battleship SMS Posen

KAGERO

Starboard view of the German Battleship SMS *Posen*, 1910.

SMS *Posen*

The last ship of the first class of German "Dreadnought" battleships was *Ersatz Baden/Posen*. The keel for *Posen* was laid on 11 June 1907 at the Germania Dockyard in Kiel and launching followed on 12 December 1908. The President of the Prussian province of Posen, von Waldow, gave the christening speech and the christening was performed by Fürstin (Princess) Johanna von Radolin. *Posen* was named after the Prussian Province from 1772 to 1919, and today is known as Poznan province in Poland. On 28 April 1910 *Posen* was transferred from her construction yard to Kiel Imperial Dockyard and on 31 May was commissioned for the first time. The first pre-trials began on 18 July 1910.

Specifications

Ersatz Baden	Posen
Construction Dockyard	Germania Dockyard, Kiel
Building number	132
Contract	13.11.1906
Keel laying	11.6.1907
Launched	12.12.1908
Completed	28.4.1910
Commissioned	31.5.1910
Cost (million Marks)	36.92
Displacement (tonnes)	Designed: 18.873 / Loaded: 20.535
Length in CWL	145.6m
Beam	26.9m
Draught	8.57m
Moulded depth	13.25m
Performance	Designed: 22.000 iHP / Maximum: 28.117 iHP
Revolutions	Designed: 117 Maximum: 127
Speed (knots)	Designed: 19.0 knots / Maximum: 20.12 knots
Fuel (tonnes) From 1915:	950 coal / 2977 coal Fuel oil: 160
Range (NM/knots)	9.400 at 10 knots
Compartments	16
Crew	40 Officers, 968 men

Hull

Posen was constructed of Siemens-Martin mild steel (ship building steel) with transverse bulkheads and longitudinal frames.

There was a double side and bottom from frame 12 to 16 on the side of the shaft tunnels, from frame 16 to 21 it extended between the keel and longitudinal frame II and from 21 to 99 was between the keel and armoured deck. From frame 99 to frame 108 the double side extended only as far as the lower platform deck. The double bottom extended over 88% of the ship.

Fifteen watertight compartments divided the ship into 16 watertight compartments.

From frame 32 to 67 there was a wing passage bulkhead which extended from the inner bottom to the armoured deck, and from frame 21 to 86 there was a torpedo bulkhead which passed through the inner bottom.

The engine rooms were divided by two longitudinal bulkheads between frames 32 and 41, which reached from the inner bottom to the armoured deck.

Below the armoured deck in the middle of the ship, between frames 41 and 75, was a 1.45m wide middle gangway, in which ran the steering controls, the engine telegraphs, electrical cables, speaking tubes, fire extinguisher lines and compressed air pipes etc. The middle gangway ran through all bulkheads and between frames 63 and 66, where the central command position was located, it was increased in width to 3m.

Between frames 21 and 75 on the armoured deck were the coal provisions upper bunkers, and the reserve bunkers from frame 23 to 41 on the Zwischendeck. Below the armoured deck were the ready use bunkers of the boiler rooms, inside the torpedo bulkheads. Outside the torpedo bulkhead were the protective bunkers.

The ship had the following decks: Stauung or hold, which strictly speaking was not a deck, Lower Platform Deck, Upper Platform Deck, Zwischendeck or Between deck, Armoured Deck, Batterie Deck, Upper

Deck and Superstructure Deck. The decks were of steel plate. The exposed part of the Batterie Deck and the Upper Deck were covered with 60 mm thick teak planking, whilst all remaining decks were covered in linoleum.

Armour

The upper deck of *Posen* above the casemates had 25 mm thick armour and the Battery Deck was also 25 mm thick

The Armoured Deck extended from Frame -5 to the stem. Aft it was 60 mm thick, but 65 mm above the rudder engines and spindle drives. For the length of the citadel, it was 40 mm thick. The sloping armoured deck was 52 mm thick. Before and aft of the citadel the armoured deck generally 37 mm thick.

The upper edge of the side armour was the batterie deck and the lower edge was 1.6m below the CWL. In the area of the citadel the belt had a thickness of 290mm. The upper part of the belt, the so-called citadel, varied but in general was 250 mm thick, whilst the upper part which continued to the upper deck and contained the casemates, was 160 mm thick. The armour was mounted on a backing of 50 mm thick wood.

The stern armour aft of the citadel was in general 120 mm thick, whilst the bow armour between frame 86 and 108 was 140 mm, and from frame 108 to the stem was 100 mm thick. All armour was manufactured from hardened nickel steel.

As mentioned the casemate armour formed a continuation of the citadel armour up to the Upper Deck and was 160 mm thick.

The longitudinal splinter bulkheads were 15 mm thick whilst the transverse splinter bulkheads were 20 mm thick.

The six turrets were mounted two on the centreline, and four side turrets in wing positions. The barbette of the I midship turret in the bow, had hardened nick steel armour 280, 250 and 200 mm in thickness. The II midship turret barbette (aft) had an armoured thickness of 250 and 200 mm thickness. The rotating turrets had a face thickness of 280 mm, a rear of 260 mm and side thickness of 220mm. The front part of the sloping turret roof was 90 mm thick and the roof was 60 mm thick.

The 15 cm cannon had a shield 80 mm thick whilst the 8.8 cm guns had shields 50 mm thick.

The upper forward conning tower was 400 mm thick on the front and sides, and 300 mm thick aft. The interior partitions were 60 mm thick and the door had a thickness of 100mm. The roof was 80 mm and the bottom was 50 mm thick.

The lower part of the forward conning tower had front and sides 250 mm thick, and was 150 mm thick aft. Inside the conning tower the shaft had a thickness of 70 mm, whilst outside it was 100 mm thick down to the armoured deck.

The aft conning tower likewise had hardened nickel steel armour. The thickness was 200 mm with a 100 mm thick door. The roof and bottom were 50 mm and the tube for the command elements was 120 mm thick.

The torpedo bulkhead varied in thickness from 20 to 30mm.

Armament

Posen mounted twelve 28 cm SK of a new type. The barrel length was increased from L/40 to L/45, whilst the longer barrel was lighter and capable of better performance. At the same time the weight of the cradle was reduced. A muzzle velocity of 871 m.p.s could be achieved. Trials were also conducted with the new powder R.P. C/07, which had reduced percentage of nitroglycerine (15%) compared to R.P. C/06 powder and although muzzle velocity was slightly reduced in the first trials to approximately 830 m.p.s the barrel wear was also reduced. Barrel life was around 200 shots. The required performance was firing a 305 kg shell with an initial muzzle velocity of 850 metres per second with a gas pressure of not above 3000 atmospheres. This was achieved consistently with C/07 powder.

The wing turrets had fixed ammunition elevators which brought the ammunition from the upper platform deck, lower platform deck or hold to the batterie deck, where it was transferred to elevators which rotated with the turrets.

Posen had the cartridge rooms for the forward and aft centreline turrets were on the Upper Platform Deck and the shell rooms were on the Lower Platform Deck. For the wing turrets the cartridge rooms were on the Lower Platform Deck, whilst the shells rooms were on the hold.

The turret training arcs for the turrets were as follows:
Forward centreline turret A: 140° – 220°
Starboard wing turret B: 155° – 355°
Starboard wing turret C: 25° – 185°
Aft centreline turret D: 40° – 320°
Port wing turret E: 175° – 335°
Port wing turret F: 205° – 5°

The 28cm SK L/45 could fire at a maximum rate of fire of 3 shots per minute. Maximum elevation was +20° and depression -6°, giving a maximum range of 18.900m, which was improved to 20.400m in 1915. Only armour piercing shells were carried with a total of 75 shots per gun. These weighed 305kg. The 'new' 28cm shell was capped to give increased performance. Trials at the testing range at Meppen revealed the 'new' shell could penetrate 280mm of nickel steel plate at a range of 10.000m, and 200mm of nickel steel plate at 12.000m.

The shell was propelled at an initial muzzle velocity of 850 metres per second (up to 877mps on trials) by a fore charge and main charge with a total of 105kg of RP C/12 propellant. The tubular propellant, RP C/12, consisted of the fore charge which came in a silk bag and weighed 26kg. The main charge, consisting of 79kg of propellant, came in a brass cartridge case. The brass case sealed the breech and proved to be fire resistant under combat conditions.

There was a total of eight range finders, one in each conning tower, and one on each turret.

The secondary, or medium artillery consisted of 12 – 15cm cannon in battery deck casemates in M.P.L. C/1906 mountings (*Mittel Pivot Lafette*, or medium pivot mounting). As originally mounted these cannon had an elevation of +20° and depression of -7°, allowing a range of 13.500 metres. Later this range was increased to 16.800m. A rate of fire of 6–8 shots per minute could be achieved. The guns crew consisted of eight men. Each gun carried two telescopes for sighting. As with the heavy artillerie the munition was split, the shell weighing 45.3kg and having an initial muzzle velocity of 835 mps. The cartridge weighed 22.6kg, and carried a load of 13.7kg of propellant. For each gun there were 50 armour piercing shells and 100 head fused high explosive shells.

There were five 15cm ammunition chambers on the upper platform deck, of them two each to port and starboard amidships, and one to port aft. There were five ammunition chambers on the lower platform deck, two each to port and starboard forward, and one to starboard aft. In addition there were four ammunition chambers on the hold, two each to port and starboard. There were 12 ammunition shafts with chain hoists, one for each gun.

To defend against attack from torpedoboat-destroyers an armament of 16 – 8.8cm SK L/45 cannon, mounted in M.P.L. C/1906 mounts was carried. The 8.8cm gun was a powerful piece, and the shell and cartridge came in one piece. The total weight was 15.5kg, and the 10kg shell could be propelled with an initial muzzle velocity of 750 metres per second. With a maximum elevation of +25°, and a depression of -10°, the maximum range was a respectable 10.700 metres. The rate of fire was quoted at 25–30 shots per minute and the crew comprised three men. One crewman operated the elevating and traversing gear, one man set the sights and the last man was a loader. For each gun there were 75 head fused high explosive shells and 75 other high explosive shells, making a total of 150 shots per gun and 2400 shots total on board. To store the ammunition there were five chambers on the upper platform deck, one each to port and starboard forward, and one amidships, and one each to port and starboard aft, the port aft also being a 15cm munition chamber. A total of eight elevators brought the ammunition to the guns.

During the course of the war two of on the aft superstructure 8.8cm SK were replaced by two 8.8cm Flak L/45 in the M.P.L. C/1913 mount. These guns likewise fired a shell weighing 10kg, and were manned by a 5 man crew. Initial muzzle velocity was again 750mps, but the elevation was increased from 20° to 70°.

In the Reiches Marine Amt it was believed that a battle would soon resolve itself to a close range action, and therefore German battleships carried a powerful torpedo armament. *Posen* was outfitted with a total of six torpedo tubes, one each in the bow and stern, and four firing on the broadside. The bow tube was fixed in the stem and fired directly ahead and the forward broadside tubes were on the lower platform deck in the torpedo room to port and starboard. The aft broadside torpedo room was located on the lower platform deck The stern torpedo tube fired directly aft.

An outfit of 16 – 45cm C/06 torpedoes was carried. These torpedoes had a diameter of 450mm and a length of 5650mm, weighed 800kg and carried a warhead weighing 120kg. At 30 knots they had a range of 2000 metres, and at 36 knots a range of 1000m. The torpedo rooms were, of necessity, comparatively large and took up a considerable space below the armoured deck.

Machinery

Posen had three triple expansion engines each with three cylinders. The engines were designed to provide 20.000 iHP with approximately 117 rpm, for a speed of 19 knots, although as with all German capital ships

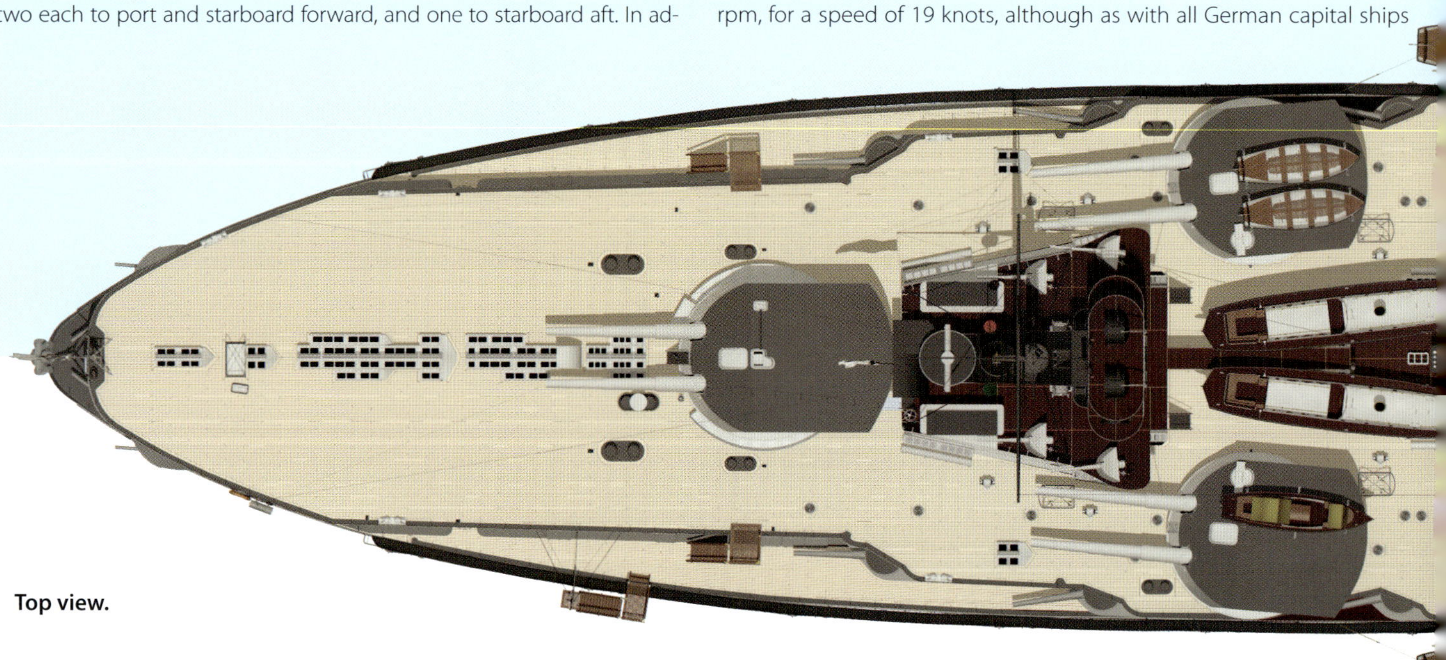

Top view.

the figures were exceeded during trials. A forced draught of 65 mm air pressure could be provided.

The ship was driven by three 4 bladed propellers each of 5m diameter. The starboard propeller rotated to the right, the port and middle propellers to the left.

Steam was provided by 12 Naval boilers manufactured by the construction yard. There were three boiler rooms, each divided into two by a longitudinal bulkhead. The boilers had a total of 24 fires and total heating area of 5040 square metres. Steam was produced at a pressure of 16 atmospheres, or 235 psi. Either natural or forced draught could be employed.

Construction coal provisions were 950 tonnes and a maximum of 2968 tonnes could be carried when using the reserve bunkers. After the installation of supplemental oil firing in 1915 160 tonnes of tar oil was provided.

There were two rudders mounted in parallel. Each was driven by a steam driven spindle drive.

The manoeuvrability of SMS *Posen* was very good. The speed loss with hard rudder and high speed was quite substantial, so that with turns caution had to be used. The arrangement of two rudder blades adjacent to one another proved very satisfactory. Quite apart from the advantage of a reserve it also allowed the ship to have a very small turning circle. With 12 knots speed and 35° rudder the diameter of the circle was only 320 metres, whereby nevertheless, a considerable loss in speed was expected. The list of the ship with hard rudder totalled 2°.

Based on the results of the coal measuring trial on 2 October 1910 with a coal provision of 2977 tonnes and a speed of 12 knots the ship has a range of approximately 8460 nautical miles.

The accommodation of the crew was generally good.

The trials report concluded: "The overall construction and performance of all mechanical equipment is satisfactory and can be described as quite good. The entire machinery can be seen by its performance and efficiency as a success.

By and large SMS *Posen* is thus considered a quite successful ship that may be considered as a valuable asset to the Navy by virtue of its powerful armament and strong armour, as well as his high speed."

Operational Career

Commanders 31 May 1910 to 16 December 1918:

Kapitän zur See Back	5.10–9.12
Kapitän zur See Lange (Richard)	10.12–6.17
Kapitän zur See Krosigk (Wilhelm)	6.17–11.18
Korvettenkapitän Zirzow (Otto)	11.18
Unoccupied	11.18–12.18

The trials were completed by 27 August 1910 and on 7 September *Posen* arrived in Wilhelmshaven and the crew was reduced. When *Wittelsbach* was de-commissioned on 20 September the crew of *Posen* was filled out and she was officially incorporated into the High Sea Fleet. In November 1910 *Posen* took part in the manoeuvres and training of the I Squadron for the first time and participated in all training up until the beginning of the war.

In 1911 *Posen* received arrangements for a Division Staff and then served as flagship for the 2 Admiral of the I Squadron. In March 1911 Fleet exercises took place in the Skagerrak and Kattegat. After hosting British and American ships visiting Kiel in June *Posen* joined in the July and August manoeuvres after which the summer cruise of the High Sea Fleet to Norway took place. The autumn exercises took place in the Kattegat and western Baltic. After the spring manoeuvres in 1912 the summer cruise went to the western Baltic. The autumn manoeuvres were north of Helgoland.

In March 1913 the I Squadron undertook exercises in the North Sea followed by further exercises in April and then Fleet manoeuvres in the North Sea in May. In the second half of July and first days of August the fleet undertook a summer cruise to Norwegian waters. On the last day of August the autumn manoeuvres began off Helgoland and then unit training and Fleet exercises followed in October and November 1913.

The year 1914 began as the previous year and at the end of March the spring manoeuvres took place in the North Sea. In April and May fleet manoeuvres took place in the Baltic and North Sea. Despite the assassination of the successor to the Austrian throne, Archduke Franz Ferdinand and his wife on 28 June, the High Sea Fleet continued preparations for its summer cruise. On 13 July 1914 the last peacetime cruise of the fleet began and exercises followed in the area of Skagen. On 25 July the ships ran into Norwegian fjords in units, but by the evening of 26 July they had already quit their anchorages because meanwhile Austro-Hungary had delivered an ultimatum to the Serbians and the political situation had become dire. On 27 July the entire High Sea Fleet met at the appointed rendezvous on the latitude of Cape Skudenes. By 29 July the High Sea Fleet had reached its bases at Wilhelmshaven and Kiel.

On 1 August 1914 *Posen* stood in Wilhelmshaven Roads when the order for mobilisation arrived. At 1800hrs on 3 August a telegram arrived announcing war with France and the following day Britain declared war on Germany. Supplies, including ammunition, were replenished. Exercises followed on 7 August followed by shooting practice the following day. On 28 August *Posen* put to sea as one of the ships of a counter thrust against British forces that had attacked cruisers in the Helgoland Bight.

On 2 November the I Squadron weighed anchor and put to sea to support the raid on Yarmouth. On the evening of 3 November 1914 conditions in the German Bight were poor with reduced visibility and

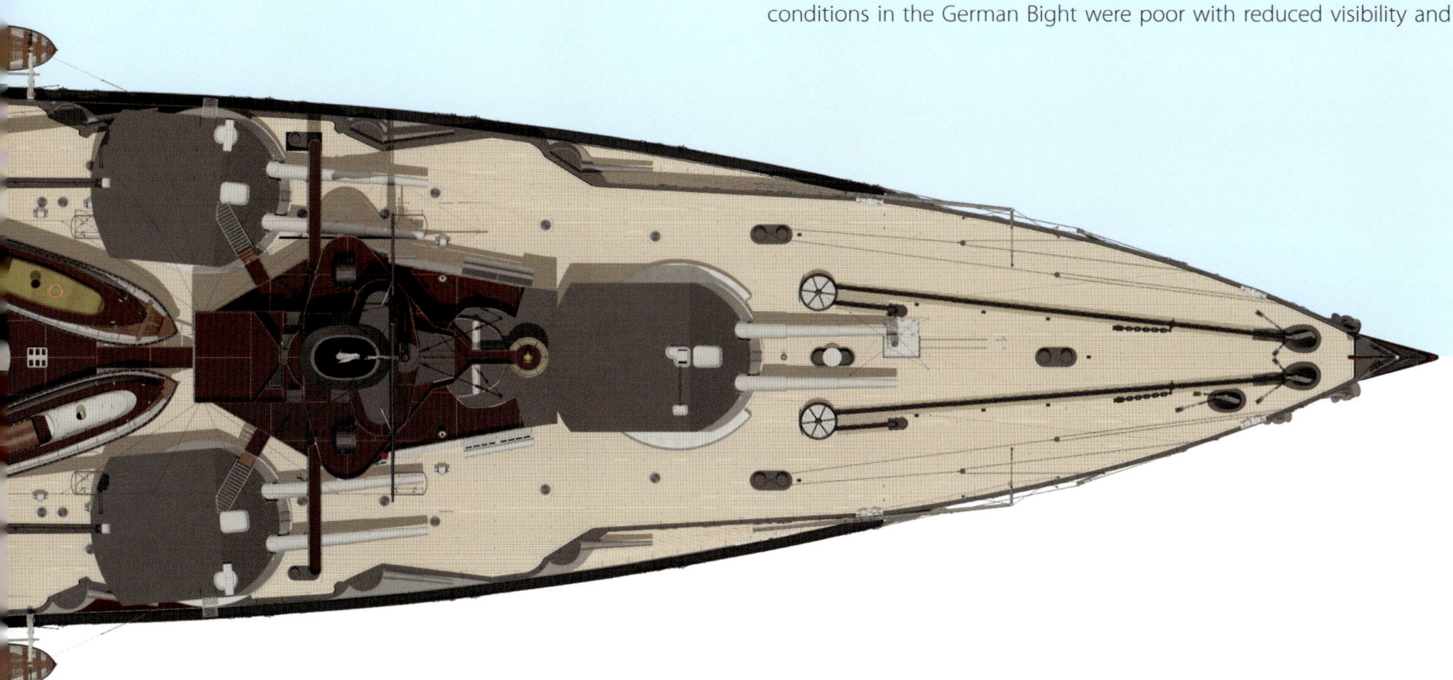

The German Battleship SMS *Posen*, 1910.
Port side view.

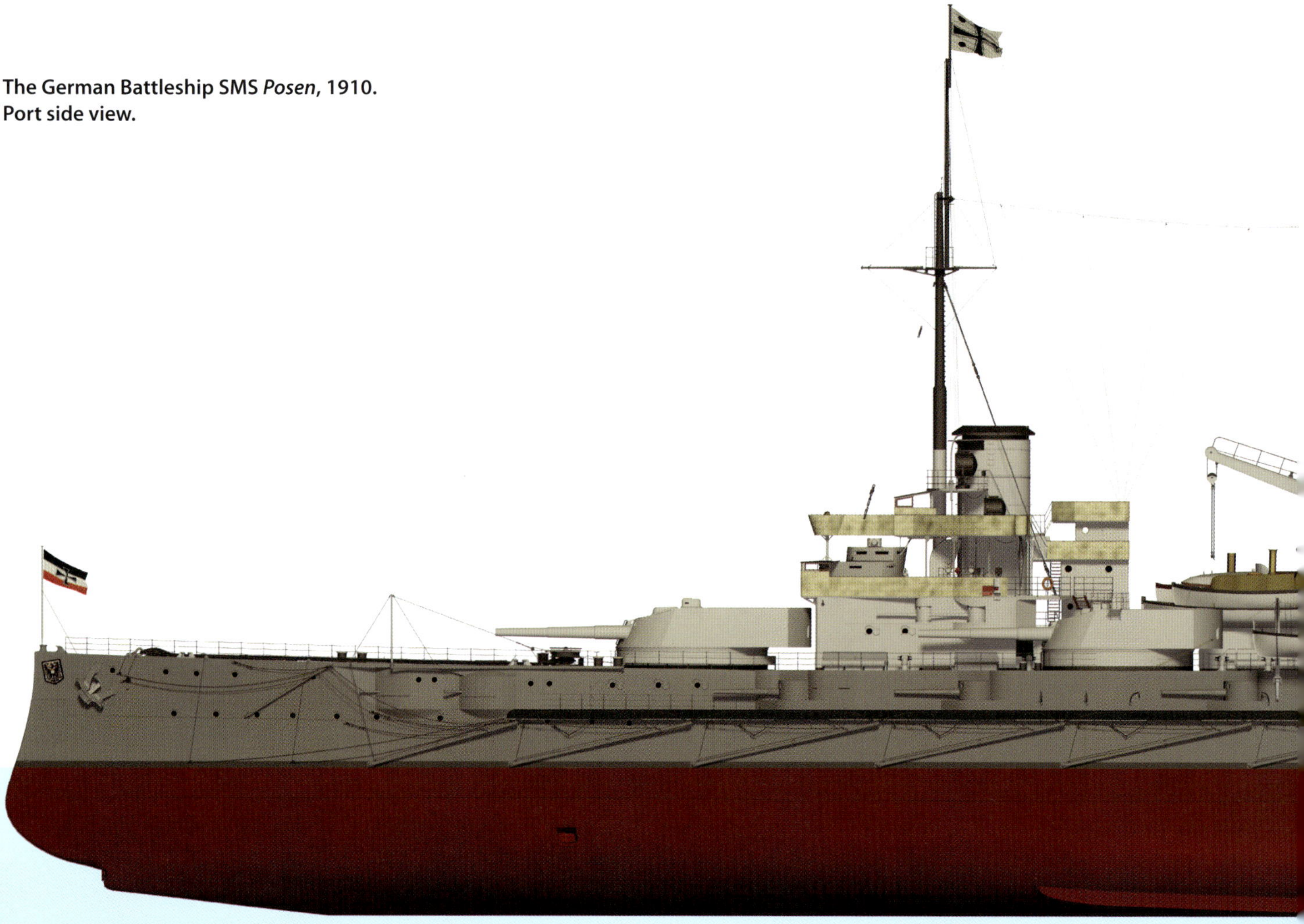

the I Squadron was detached to the Elbe river, where *Posen* anchored. The following day *Posen* remained anchored on the Elbe as fog dominated and only on 5 November did the ship anchor on Wilhelmshaven Roads in rain.

On 15 December the I Squadron put to sea as part of the High Sea Fleet in accordance with operational order 20, the bombardment of Scarborough, Whitby and Hartlepool by the I AG. Once again the bombardment was only a secondary objective, the main purpose was to provoke the British into countering with some part of their naval forces, which would be cut off and attacked by the Fleet. This plan succeeded very well and at the following morning *Posen* sighted a series of muzzle flashes and then the recognition signal was exchanged with the small cruiser *Hamburg*. *Hamburg* was firing on an enemy destroyer, upon which several hits were observed. The destroyer belonged to the vanguard of a British force consisting of 1 Battlecruiser Squadron, 2 Battle Squadron, 3 Cruiser Squadron and 1 Light Cruiser Squadron. British naval intelligence had become aware of the German operation and had dispatched these forces to sea to intercept them. However, the British plan had backfired and their forces were trapped between Kontreadmiral Hipper's I AG and the High Sea Fleet. However, upon first contact with the British light forces the High Sea Fleet chief, Admiral von Ingenohl, turned away therefore leaving Kontreadmiral Hipper unsupported. Now it was the German battlecruisers that were cut off. To escape the trap the I AG had to detour around the northern edge of the Dogger Bank. Ingenohl had missed a wonderful opportunity to reduce the superior numbers of the British Grand Fleet.

On the morning of 22 February the I Squadron weighed anchor and set course for the Elbe, speed 17 knots. As a thick fog suddenly came up the ships anchored near the Elbe light vessel before resuming their trip, however anchored a short time later near the Elbe B light vessel. The thick fog persisted all the next day. Only at on 24 February could the journey be resumed. More thick fog interrupted the trip. A period of training in Kiel followed with target ship shooting, torpedo firing and searchlight training, Flak shooting, Unit training and night firing exercises. On 12 March *Posen* anchored on Schillig Roads, bringing to a close a successful training period in the Baltic.

Admiral von Ingenohl had missed a wonderful opportunity on 16 December 1914 and then he had planned the operation that led to the Dogger Bank battle and loss of SMS *Blücher*, therefore he was relieved from his position as Fleet Chief early in February 1915 and was replaced by Admiral von Pohl. Concurrent with the appointment of Admiral Pohl was the declaration of the waters around Great Britain as a war zone, therefore beginning the first unrestricted submarine campaign. The first fleet operation under von Pohl took place on 29 March 1915.

On 17 April 1915 *Posen* supported a minelaying operation by the small cruisers *Stralsund* and *Straßburg* on the Swarte Bank. After supporting the minelaying operation the fleet returned to the Helgoland Bight where they carried out evolutions from on 18 April, then *Posen* returned to Wilhelmshaven Roads and anchored.

On 6 May *Posen* entered dock for an overhaul period. Then on 29 May the I Squadron departed Schillig Roads together with the III and II Squadrons as cover for the auxiliary cruiser *Meteor* which was putting to sea to lay mines in the White Sea off the Russian coast.

On 31 July *Posen* ran into Wilhelmshaven and secured at berth 4 for the installation of two B.A.K. On the morning of 3 August 1915 *Posen* put to sea and steered to the Elbe for the canal trip to the east. The I Squadron was placed under the authority of the Commander in Chief of the Baltic, Großadmiral Prinz Heinrich. The purpose of the operation into the Baltic was to support the break-in to the Gulf of Riga. The battleships were to steer to the west of Ösel Island and counter any operation by the new Russian dreadnought battleships to disrupt the break-in attempt. In command of the operation was the High Command or *Oberleitung*, Vizeadmiral Ehrhard Schmidt, the commander of the IV Squadron.

On 4 August *Posen* arrived in Kiel. On 6 August *Posen* ran out of Kiel in accordance with operational orders and proceeded east at 14 knots. The following day the centre engine suffered damage. The

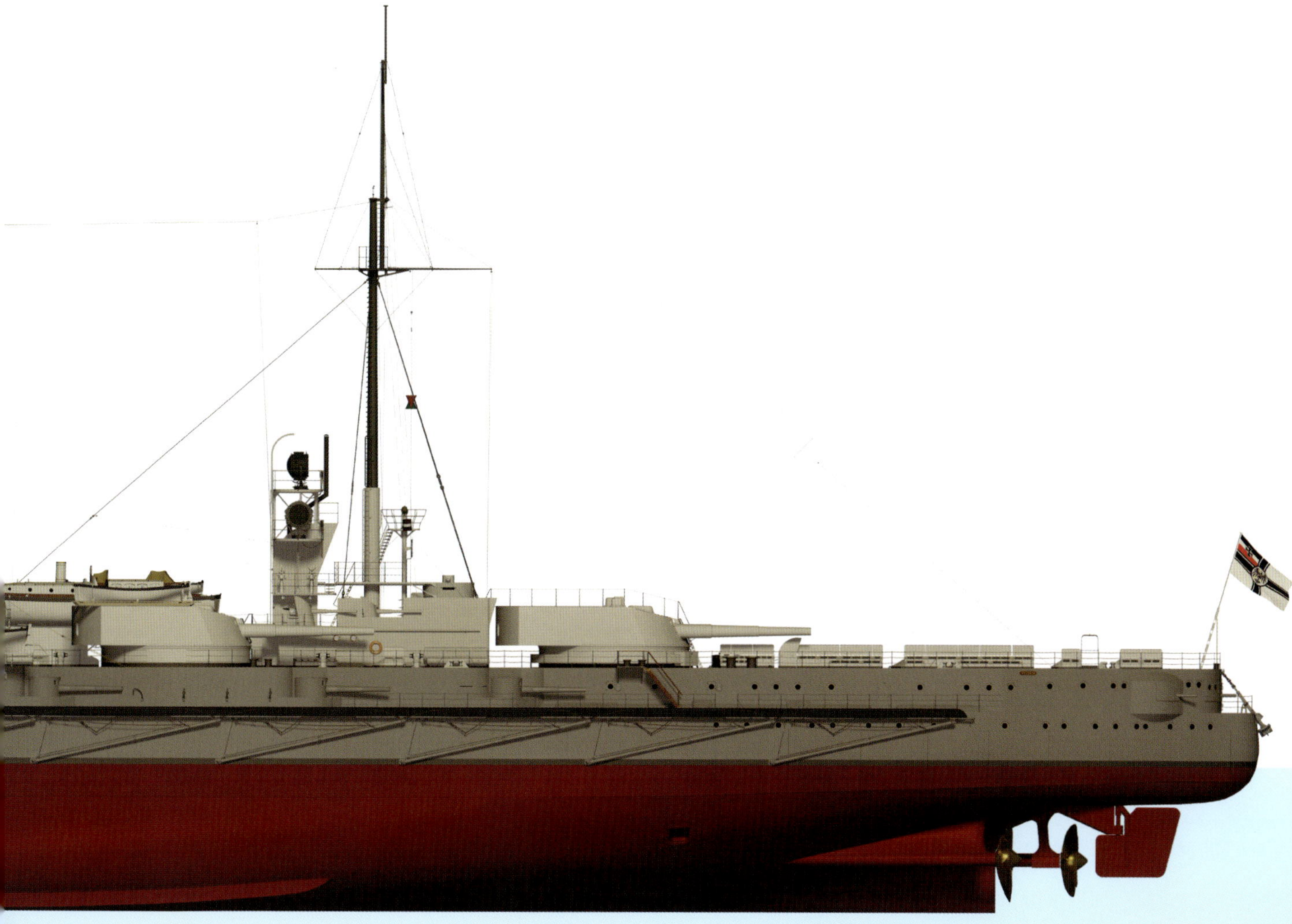

medium pressure slide push rod broke so that the centre engine had to be uncoupled to allow repairs. After 45 minutes the uncoupling was effected so that with the side engines *Posen* could rejoin the Squadron, which had come back in sight on the opposite course.

On 8 August *Posen* stopped briefly to begin recoupling of the centre engine. The recoupling took approximately 35 minutes and *Posen* proceeded at slow speed with the side engines during this time. The main assault on the Riga Gulf took place on the morning of 8 August during which the battleships *Elsaß* and *Braunschweig* fired on the Russian battleship *Slava* and the gunboat *Chrabry*.

Nevertheless, the duration of the minesweeping work came as a surprise, as based upon pre-war practice it was estimated it would take three hours, but with the discovery of further mine barriers this time increased and threw the German plan schedule into disarray. Delays meant the immediate support ships would spend the night exposed to attack from submarines and therefore, after due consultation with his Staff, Vizeadmiral Schmidt suspended the operation.

From the 9 August to 11 August *Posen* and the I Squadron, remained cruising off the Riga Gulf. On 11 August *Posen* received orders to go to Kiel to replenish coal, as only 7000 tonnes were available in Swinemünde. The following morning *Posen* made fast in Kiel and 1400 tonnes of coal was taken aboard. In the evening *Posen* cast off and set course for Swinemünde, arriving there on 13 August. On 14 August *Posen* quit Swinemünde and ran out to sea as part of the I Squadron. The following day was spent cruising off the Riga Gulf. That evening *Posen* and *Nassau* were detached from the Squadron and the High Command, Vizeadmiral Schmidt, boarded *Posen*. The break-in attempt was to be repeated using the more battle worthy ships *Posen* and *Nassau*, and the old battleships of the IV Squadron were detached. Sea mastery of the Riga Gulf was seen as important as was the laying of mines in the Moon Sound exit. The destruction of *Slava* now became an important aim. However, now the Germans forces would advance further south through the Irben Straits.

On August 16 *Posen* and *Nassau* began the advance steering behind minesweepers. Progress behind the II Mine Sweeper Division was slow and tense. In the early afternoon the masts and funnels of *Slava* came in sight, and after that the minelayer *Amur*. The order was immediately given, "Clear ship for battle", and then *Posen* anchored. The High Commander, Vizeadmiral Schmidt, gave the order "Jot Dora", or open fire. Fire was inaugurated at 194hm, whereon *Slava* turned away to the NE. Fire was ceased at a range of 204cm. Sixteen shots were fired in four salvos. *Slava* replied with two salvos. At 1500hrs *Slava* again approached and opened fire on the minesweepers, so at 1519hrs *Posen* opened fire at 180hm even though the Russian could only be made out poorly. *Posen* ceased fire at a range of 204hm. *Nassau* briefly joined in the firing. *Slava* turned away and retired to the north east, but then turned back towards the German forces and renewed fire on the minesweepers. At 1615hrs *Posen* again opened fire at 204hm but ceased fire after just four minutes. Meanwhile *Slava* had taken the small cruiser *Bremen* and minesweepers under fire. At 1647hrs, under conditions of poor visibility, *Posen* took the Russian battleship under fire for the last time for the day, ceasing fire at 1653hrs. *Slava* sailed off to the NNE and spent the night in Arensburg.

The following morning, 17 August, in conditions of good visibility and light rain *Posen* recovered her torpedo nets and weighed anchor. *Posen* remained in the channel buoyed by the minesweepers and advanced. *Posen* observed several Russian destroyers in the ENE and in deteriorating conditions, with haze and visibility of just 6 nautical miles, *Posen* opened fire on these with her medium calibre artillerie at a range of 105hm. As the weather cleared somewhat *Slava* came in sight at a range of 194hm and five minutes later *Posen* opened fire with her heavy cannon. As the range increased to 204 cm fire was ceased. *Posen* recovered her torpedo nets and went at slow speed in the buoyed channel. Once again *Slava* came in sight and was fired upon between 0745 and 0756hrs. It was believed that a hit was irreproachably observed on the Russian battleship amidships.

At 0800hrs *Posen* anchored in the swept channel because the I and II Minesweeper Divisions reported closely spaced mine barriers.

On 8 August *Slava* did not open fire on the German battleships as she did not want to reveal that her 12 inch guns were outranged by the German 28cm pieces. To increase her range *Slava* hastily improvised a system of flooding three wing passage compartments to heel the ship 3° and therefore increase the range of her cannon. This procedure took 10–15 minutes. On 8 August *Slava* received no hits but her decks were showered with 28cm shell splinters.

On 16 August *Slava's* targets included torpedobootes, minesweepers and *Posen* and *Nassau*. In total *Slava* made 16 salvo`s firing 35 – 12 inch and 20 – 6 inch shells.

On the morning of 17 August *Slava* weighed anchor and, escorted by destroyers of the VIII Division, moved to the firing position at full speed. There was a heavy mist and fog and at first the battleship could not see the Germans. At 0620hrs the ship saw muzzle flashes, and then the fall of German shells near her destroyer escorts. The battle flags were raised and the battleship moved south on the meridian of Zerel. Visibility to the west continued to be 40-50 cable lengths (73 to 91hm). The Germans concentrated their fire on *Slava*, although their ships were not visible. After several shots the shells began to get closer and at 0648hrs, after 5 shots, the fire was ceased. *Slava* went onto an easterly course, moving out of the range of the German fire. At 0740hrs the rangefinder of *Slava* saw German torpedobootes and minesweepers near the lighthouse at Pissen at a range of about 85-90 cables (155–165hm). The battleship was still unable to open fire because the turrets could still not see the target. Five minutes later the German dreadnoughts opened fire at great range and *Slava* turned north at full speed. Almost immediately afterwards *Slava* was hit by three 28cm shells at the same time. The steering control immediately failed and the ship was steered by the engines. *Posen* and *Nassau* continued to straddle *Slava* but at 0756 ceased firing after 12 salvos. The ship quickly coped with fires and damage to the steering gear, and in relation to the risk of fire the aft port 6 inch magazine was flooded. There were no dead or wounded, however some men suffered burns. Despite wanting to continue the fight *Slava* was ordered to Arensburg. On this day fire could not be opened because of the fog and haze.

The following day, 18 August, was mainly spent by *Posen* edging forward behind the minesweepers before anchoring during the afternoon.

Early on the morning of 19 August the German battleships were ordered to get steam up in all boilers. The original main aim of the operation had been to support the Armee on their seaward flank as they advanced against Riga, but there were also secondary objectives, such as the auxiliary minelayer *Deutschland* blockading the Moon Sound, and sinking blockships in the entrance to Pernau harbour. At midday on 19 August the cruisers carried out reconnaissance according to plan: *Bremen* went to Arensburg, *Pillau* to the eastern bays of Ösel, *Augsburg* to Pernau and *Graudenz* went to the narrows between Domesnas and Runö. During the evening of 19 August *Augsburg*, together with torpedobootes *V29* and *V100*, was returning to the Main Body when about 1900hrs *Augsburg* sighted two vessels in the W by N. The vessels were given the recognition signal several times but failed to answer so at 1945hrs *Augsburg* opened fire. In the evening twilight the fall of shot could not be observed and fire was ceased, whilst a contact report was sent to *Posen*. At 1956hrs the two vessels were made out as Russian gunboats, *Sivuch* and *Korietz*. These two gunboats had been based in Dünamünde and had shelled German Armee positions three times and laid mines, but now were returning to the Moon Sound under the cover of darkness. During this phase of the battle *Augsburg* was hit twice, once on the hull side at frame 92 and once on the forecastle, which put the foremast searchlight out of action.

Previously, at 1730hrs, the Main Body had reached the southern exit of Moon Sound, but because of deteriorating weather, the gathering dark and the presence of Russian destroyers the minelaying had to be left undone and Vizeadmiral Schmidt turned away to the south for the night. At 1945hrs *Posen* received *Augsburg's* contact report and at 2005hrs gunfire was observed to port and ahead. At 2010hrs the recognition signal was exchanged with *Augsburg* and at 2012hrs fire was opened on a Russian ship. Soon after *Posen* ceased fire and turned to port to bring her broadside to bear, and at 2017hrs hours turned back to starboard onto her old course. When she resumed fire it was uncertain which Russian gunboat she was now taking under fire. *Nassau* was also firing on this target at a range of only 12 to 8hm and the Russians were suffering under a murderous fire. With the fourth salvo the bow 12cm cannon of *Sivuch* was thrown overboard. Numerous fires were started and there was a boiler explosion. The German torpedobootes fired a total of six torpedoes and it was reported by Russian survivors that both gunboats were hit. At 2026hrs *Nassau* ceased fire, followed soon after by *Posen*, as *Sivuch* lay motionless and burning. At 2029hrs she capsized and sank by the bow.

Korietz was also hit and damaged however made off to the east into the darkness. The following morning upon hearing the erroneous news that Pernau was in German hands her commander ran his ship aground at Cape Merris and blew her up.

The German torpedobootes had hurried to the scene of *Sivuch* sinking and rescued 2 officers and 48 men, but unfortunately some of the wounded died enroute to Swinemünde. At 2255hrs the Main Body anchored for the night and *Posen* set her torpedo nets

On 20 August at 0345hrs 41 prisoners from *Sivuch* were taken aboard *Posen*, but were then transferred to *Nassau*. Anchor was weighed and the Main Body took course NE by E, behind the I Minesweeper Division. The remainder of the day was spent cruising about the Riga Gulf in support of the blockading of Pernau with blockships before at 1855hrs the unit anchored 3–4NM off Pissen. On the afternoon of 21 August *Posen* and *Nassau* were detached to a rendezvous with the I Squadron, and then the I squadron began the trip to Swinemünde at 15 knots. On 22 August *Posen* made fast in Swinemünde. The following day 1200 tonnes of coal was taken aboard before on 24 August *Posen* cast off and put to sea bound for Kiel, where she arrived the following day. On 26 August *Posen* ran into the Kaiser Wilhelm Canal with the I Squadron and that evening anchored in the Elbe river. The following day she weighed anchor and steered to the Jade where she anchored on Wilhelmshaven Roads.

On 11 September 1915 *Posen* weighed anchor and went to sea to support the small cruisers *Stralsund* and *Regensburg* which would lay several mine barriers near the Swarte Bank. On 30 September *Posen* ran into Dock V to have her bottom cleaned and a propeller blade replaced.

In clear moonshine on 23 October *Posen* weighed anchor and put to sea in accordance with Operational Order Nr. 31. Because of unsuitable weather airship reconnaissance was unavailable and at 0500hrs on 24 October a turn was made to retrace their path of advance. At 0853hrs it was reported that a British submarine had fired a torpedo on *Hamburg*, which, however missed. A short time later, at 0929hrs, there was a missed torpedo shot on *Rostock*, and then 20 minutes later *von der Tann* reported a torpedo track to starboard. The torpedo attacks on *Hamburg* and *Rostock* were carried out by the submarine *E6*. During the afternoon *Posen* anchored on Wilhelmshaven Roads.

During the war all German ships and units underwent comprehensive training periods in Kiel and Baltic. The value and intensity of this training can be seen by the diverse list of training activities over any period, which could include any of the following: torpedo shooting, searchlight training, serving as a target for torpedoboote attacks, battleline training, night calibre shooting against targets illuminated with star shells, range finder training, B.A.K. shooting against target balloons, calibre shooting, and damage control drills.

On 7 January 1916 *Posen* ran into the dockyard for installation of the RW artillery equipment and supplemental oil firing. Two days later she moved to Dock V for work on the ships bottom and propellers. All of this work was only concluded on 26 January and *Posen* was again combat ready.

The weather was clear with visibility 15 nautical miles when at midnight on 3 March *Posen* ran out under the command of the 2 Admiral of I Squadron in the series *von der Tann*, *Posen*, *Nassau* and *Westfalen*,

Fore view.

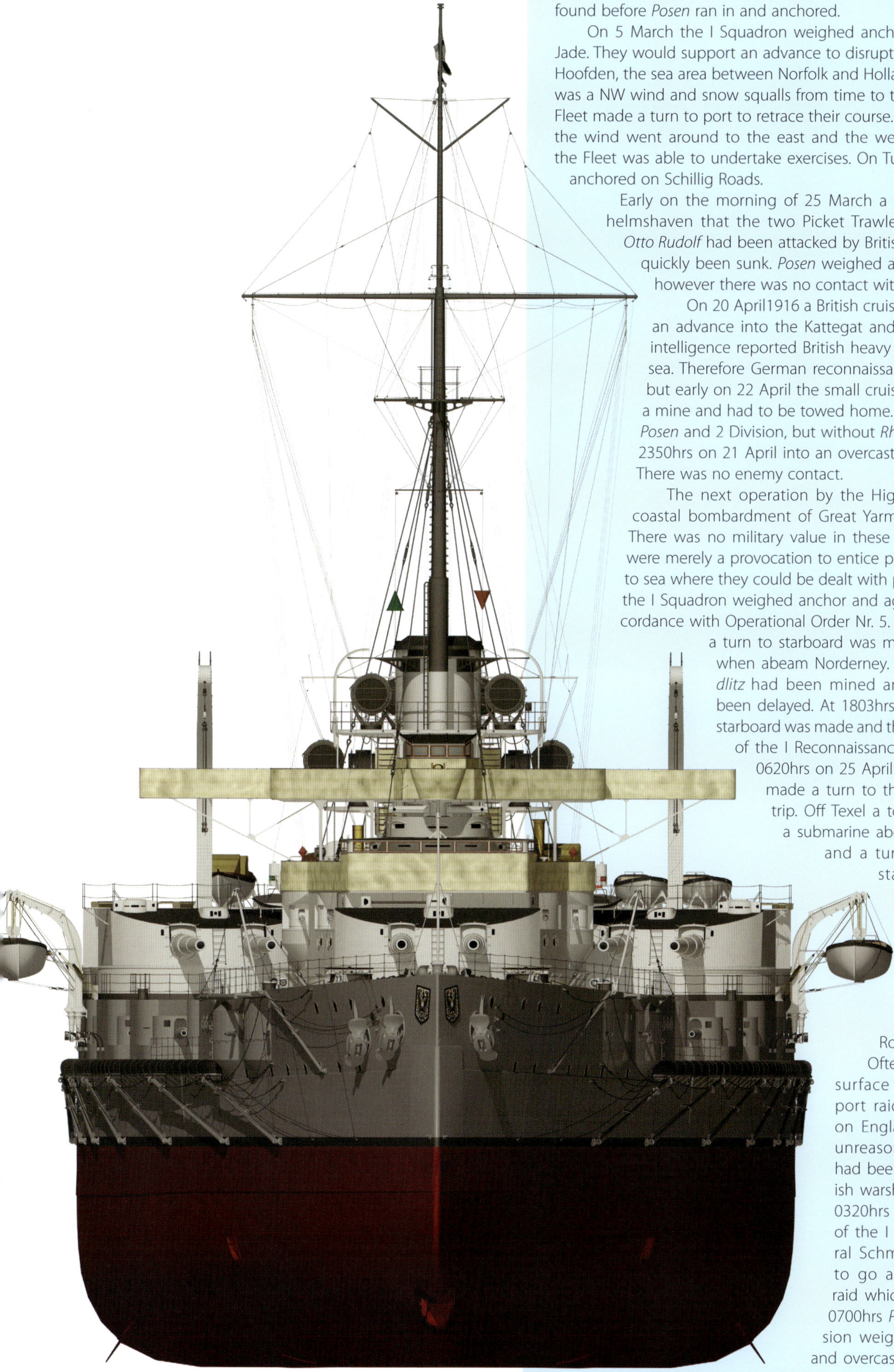

to welcome the auxiliary cruiser *Möve* home. Early on the morning of 4 March thick fog was encountered however *Möve* and the I AG were found before *Posen* ran in and anchored.

On 5 March the I Squadron weighed anchor and ran down the Jade. They would support an advance to disrupt allied shipping in the Hoofden, the sea area between Norfolk and Holland. On 6 March there was a NW wind and snow squalls from time to time as at 1030hrs the Fleet made a turn to port to retrace their course. During the afternoon the wind went around to the east and the weather cleared so that the Fleet was able to undertake exercises. On Tuesday 7 March *Posen* anchored on Schillig Roads.

Early on the morning of 25 March a report arrived in Wilhelmshaven that the two Picket Trawlers *Braunschweig* and *Otto Rudolf* had been attacked by British destroyers and had quickly been sunk. *Posen* weighed anchor and put to sea however there was no contact with British forces.

On 20 April1916 a British cruiser force put to sea for an advance into the Kattegat and on 21 April German intelligence reported British heavy units had also put to sea. Therefore German reconnaissance forces put to sea but early on 22 April the small cruiser *Graudenz* ran onto a mine and had to be towed home. To cover these forces *Posen* and 2 Division, but without *Rheinland*, put to sea at 2350hrs on 21 April into an overcast and rainy North Sea. There was no enemy contact.

The next operation by the High Sea Fleet was the coastal bombardment of Great Yarmouth and Lowestoft. There was no military value in these bombardments, they were merely a provocation to entice part of the Grand Fleet to sea where they could be dealt with piecemeal. At 1345hrs the I Squadron weighed anchor and again put to sea in accordance with Operational Order Nr. 5. During the afternoon a turn to starboard was made back to the east when abeam Norderney. The battlecruiser *Seydlitz* had been mined and the advance had been delayed. At 1803hrs and further turn the starboard was made and the advance in support of the I Reconnaissance Group resumed. At 0620hrs on 25 April the battle squadrons made a turn to the ENE for the return trip. Off Texel a torpedoboot reported a submarine abeam the III Squadron and a turn away 8 points to starboard was made. There were more submarine alarms and further manoeuvring away to starboard. That evening *Posen* anchored on Schillig Roads.

Often the High Sea Fleet surface forces would support raids by naval airships on England, which was not unreasonable since airships had been shot down by British warships. Therefore about 0320hrs on 3 May the Chief of the I Squadron, Vizeadmiral Schmidt received orders to go and support the air raid which was underway. At 0700hrs *Posen* and the 2 Division weighed anchor in hazy and overcast weather. After proceeding west at 15 knots at 1055hrs a 16 point turn to starboard was carried out to proceed to the east then north to the reported position of the airships. At 1540hrs a turn was made to return to the Jade.

On 4 May the British conducted an operation into the North Sea to lay mines and for two aircraft tenders to launch an airstrike against German airship hangers. Around 1130hrs the airship *L7* was shot down by British light cruisers and the crew were rescued by submarine *E31*. At 0015hrs on 5 May *Posen* weighed anchor and put to sea in hazy weather, but at 0435hrs made a turn and at 0906hrs anchored on Schillig Roads.

On 31 May 1916 at 0330hrs middle European time *Posen* weighed anchor and went as part of the High Sea Fleet to the Skagerrak Battle. *Posen* was Flagship of the 2 Admiral of the I Squadron, Kontreadmiral Engelhardt, and led the 2 Division. At 1607hrs the signal "Clear ship for battle" was received. At 1740hrs five enemy light cruisers came in sight, followed by four capital ships. The signal for fire distribution from the right was received and then the signal open fire. *Posen* opened fire on the light cruiser furthest on the left, direction 325°, range 160 to 170hm. After a few salvos fire was ceased as several ships were firing at the same target and *Posen* did not want to make observation difficult. Ahead British destroyers could be made out and one of these with three funnels was taken under fire at 1823hrs at a range of 130hm, and was forced to turn away. At 1832hrs an apparently unmanoeuvrable destroyer was taken under fire with the medium calibre artillery at a range of 80hm. Hits were thought to have been made and after a heavy detonation the destroyer sank. The torpedobootes of the V Flottille rescued survivors. At 1847hrs the muzzle flashes of a long line were seen, however the ships could not be made out and therefore *Posen* did not open fire. At 1920hrs *Posen* observed the destruction of *Defence*, describing it as a "huge flaming mountain approximately 200m high and afterwards a strong smoke and yellowish smoke effect was observed, a powerful explosion." At 1935hrs the signal for the battle turn onto course west was received, followed at 1956hrs for the battle turn back to the east. At this stage *Posen* could see nothing of the British and at 2017hrs the signal was taken in for a battle turn to starboard, course west. Course was altered to SW at 2026hrs and then south 2055hrs. The I AG, without *Lützow*, was to port abeam of the 2 Division and under heavy fire. The impacting shells lay near the 2 Division but of the enemy ships nothing was to be seen apart from the muzzle flashes of the shooting. To bring about some relief for the I AG *Posen* opened fire in direction 270° from 2128hrsto 2135hrs.

At 0032hrs the small cruisers fired to port for a short time and the aft most cruiser stood at short range to port abeam of *Posen*. *Posen* made the recognition signal, which was not answered, but the cruiser was recognised as *Elbing*. Suddenly *Elbing* approached, apparently not recognising *Posen*. Then it was realised that *Elbing* intended to break through the German line near *Posen*. To reduce the effect of the unavoidable collision *Posen* turned hard to starboard, stopped engines and then went astern. *Elbing* was rammed at a very acute angle and *Posen* remained undamaged. Then *Posen* turned back onto the ordered course. The cruiser lay unmanoeuvrable to starboard aft of the German line and incapable of further action. About 0200hrs the torpedoboot *S53* took off 477 men, leaving only a skeleton crew aboard to attempt to save the ship. This proved impossible and when towards 0300hrs British destroyers and a cruiser were sighted *Elbing* was scuttled.

Further encounters with British destroyers followed. At 0110hrs three British destroyers were observed approaching from port aft, and the first was illuminated and taken under fire. The searchlights beam disclosed the pennant number G30, HMS *Fortune*. When illuminated *Fortune* was observed to have launched two torpedoes and *Posen* turned away to starboard to avoid them, but not before taking the second destroyer in line under fire at a range of 16 to 8hm. *Fortune* was burning and in sinking condition.

At 0125hrs it was seen that the ships of the 2 Division ahead of *Posen* had illuminated a destroyer and taken it under fire. *Posen* turned away to starboard and also took this ship under fire at a range of 10–12hm. The salvos lay well and the destroyer was set in flames and sank. The pennant number of this boat was recognised as 78, *Ardent*. At 0137hrs *Posen* took the destroyers *Petard* and *Turbulent* under fire, along with the other leading battleships, and *Petard* was hit and *Turbulent* was sunk. From *Posen* the target was veiled in smoke after fires started. Around 1500hrs on 1 June *Posen* anchored on Schillig Roads and undertook picket duty. *Posen* suffered no losses during the battle.

Posen remained on picket duty until 15 June and then spent two days in the dockyard before more picket time. On 22 June *Posen* returned to Wilhelmshaven Dockyard and on 26 June began a period of overhaul work. The overhaul work was completed on 17 July and *Posen* ran out and anchored on Wilhelmshaven Roadstead.

On the cloudy evening of 18 August 1916 *Posen* and the 2 Division weighed anchor and united with the 1 Division to put to advance to the English coast to bombard Sunderland. At 0702hrs the report was received that *Westfalen* had been torpedoed by an enemy submarine. At 1330hrs a report was received from airship *L13* about powerful enemy forces to the south east of the High Sea Fleet which had fired on the Zeppelin. *L13* was ordered to maintain contact with the British force whilst Vizeadmiral Scheer altered course to the SE towards what he thought was an isolated part of the Grand Fleet. In fact what *L13* had seen was the Harwich force consisting of light cruisers and destroyers, and which she had subsequently lost contact with because of diversions around thunderstorms. At 1712hrs a return to the German Bight was ordered as all hope of engaging the sighted British force was gone. On 20 August *Posen* anchored on Wilhelmshaven Roads.

On the evening of 18 October 1916 *Posen* weighed anchor and steered down the Jade in the Squadron Unit in accordance with Operational Order Nr. 10. The 19 October was spent cruising in the North Sea before at 0800hrs on 20 October *Posen* passed through the southern lock and ran into Wilhelmshaven harbour.

On October 22 British forces were reported in the German Bight so that *Posen* ran out and made a brief foray down the Jade before anchoring on Schillig Roadstead. The report proved to be false.

At 0418hrs on 3 November 1916 the Division weighed anchor and steered into the North Sea for exercises under the command of the 2 Admiral. On 4 November at 2212hrs news arrived that the U-Bootes *U20* and *U30* were stranded on the Danish coast and shortly after the Fleet Chief ordered the picket forces to advance to Horns Reef to support the 4 Half Flottille which was undertaking recovery work. At 0011 hrs on the morning of 5 November the 2 Division, *Posen*, *Nassau* and *Westfalen*, without *Rheinland*, weighed anchor and ran down the Jade. The 2 Division connected to the end of the III Squadron and steered according to the orders of the Chief of the III Squadron. According to the orders from *König* 16 point turns were made at 0930hrs, 1100hrs and 1300hrs. At 1307 *Großer Kurfürst* was hit by a torpedo and one minute later *Kronprinz* was also struck. At 1345hrs orders were received to run in to Hooksiel Roads where the Division anchored the following morning.

On 7 November to 12 November *Posen* was in Wilhelmshaven Dockyard for the repair of the left barrel of D turret by the dockyard.

Early on the morning of 22 December, at 0310hrs, *Posen* put to sea to go to the Elbe river and tow sistership *Nassau* free, which had run aground south of Brunsbüttel Bank whilst on her way to Hamburg. Nevertheless *Nassau* got herself free and *Posen* returned to picket duty.

The year 1917 began much as 1916 had had finished, with periods of picket duty and dockyard time, but on the 5 February *Posen* undertook a strange role, serving as an icebreaker, travelling to the outer Jade light vessels and back. The winter of 1916/1917 was particularly harsh.

Posen went to Wilhelmshaven dockyard on 19 April 1017 and made fast at berth B V. After surrendering her munition outfit *Posen* began an overhaul period. On 25 April she moved to Dock IV for work on her bottom and propellers, work which continued until 17 May when she moved to berth A VI and took on 1200 tonnes of coal. On 19 and 20 May *Posen* took on ammunition, then on 21 May she went into the floating dock for adjustment of the RW equipment, work which continued until 24 May when the ship moved to berth G8. On 27 May the work on *Posen* was finished.

Aft view.

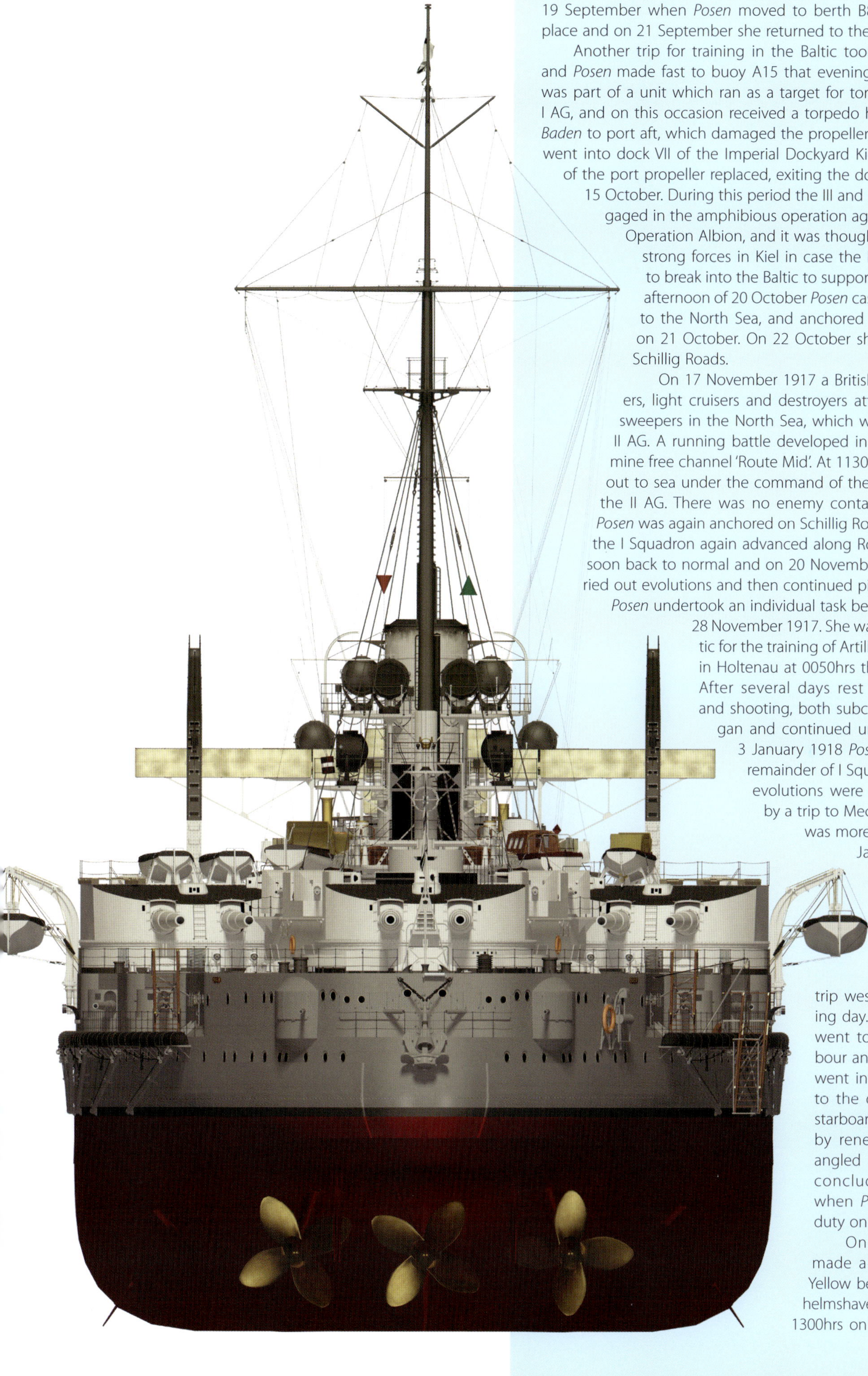

On 10 September *Posen* ran into Wilhelmshaven and went into Dock for overhaul work. The overhaul work in the dock continued until 19 September when *Posen* moved to berth B8, where coaling took place and on 21 September she returned to the roads.

Another trip for training in the Baltic took place on 7 October and *Posen* made fast to buoy A15 that evening. On 9 October *Posen* was part of a unit which ran as a target for torpedo shooting by the I AG, and on this occasion received a torpedo hit from the battleship *Baden* to port aft, which damaged the propeller. On 13 October *Posen* went into dock VII of the Imperial Dockyard Kiel to have two blades of the port propeller replaced, exiting the dock on the morning of 15 October. During this period the III and IV Squadrons were engaged in the amphibious operation against the Baltic Islands, Operation Albion, and it was thought appropriate to keep strong forces in Kiel in case the British should attempt to break into the Baltic to support the Russians. On the afternoon of 20 October *Posen* cast off for the return trip to the North Sea, and anchored on Brunsbüttel Roads on 21 October. On 22 October she finally anchored on Schillig Roads.

On 17 November 1917 a British force of battle cruisers, light cruisers and destroyers attacked German minesweepers in the North Sea, which were supported by the II AG. A running battle developed in a SE direction, in the mine free channel 'Route Mid'. At 1130hrs the I Squadron ran out to sea under the command of the 2 Admiral to support the II AG. There was no enemy contact so that at 1957hrs *Posen* was again anchored on Schillig Roads. The following day the I Squadron again advanced along Route Mid. Things were soon back to normal and on 20 November the I Squadron carried out evolutions and then continued picket duty.

Posen undertook an individual task beginning at 0740hrs on 28 November 1917. She was detached to the Baltic for the training of Artillerie Offizieres, arriving in Holtenau at 0050hrs the following morning. After several days rest a period of training and shooting, both subcalibre and calibre, began and continued until 30 December. On 3 January 1918 *Posen* was joined by the remainder of I Squadron, and then Fleet evolutions were undertaken, followed by a trip to Mecklenburg Bight. There was more Fleet training on 7–8 January 1918 and the following day *Posen* ran into Kiel harbour and made fast to buoy B1. At 1730hrs *Posen* began the canal trip west, arriving the following day. On 10 January *Posen* went to Wilhelmshaven harbour and then on 12 January went into Dock VI for repairs to the drainage pipe of the starboard 2 circulation pump by renewing of a corroded angled bracket. Repairs were concluded by 15 January when *Posen* resumed picket duty on Hooksiel Roads.

On 20 January *Posen* made a short trip on Route Yellow before returning to Wilhelmshaven harbour in rain. At 1300hrs on 23 March written orders arrived from the High Sea Chief arrived saying: "2 Admiral of the I Squadron, quickly fit out *Posen* and go to Danzig at the disposal of the Chief of Special Unit." At 1800hrs *Posen* departed for the east. On 21 February a Special Unit had been formed for the liberation of Finland from Russian and communist forces and now *Posen* was to travel east and join this unit. At 1115hrs the following day *Posen* made fast to buoy A10 in Kiel harbour and immediately began provisioning and refilling her coal stocks according to plan before departing for the east at 1900hrs. The journey continued without incident but towards midday on 25 March a strong snowstorm was encountered, together with an increasing swell and poor visibility. At 1630hrs *Posen* stood off Rixhöft and was ordered by the Chief of the Special Unit to anchor on Neufahrwasser Roads. Coaling followed. On 31 March the German transport fleet quit harbour and anchored on Neufahrwasser Roads. The following morning at 0930hrs anchor was weighed and *Posen* followed *Westfalen* to sea.

On Tuesday 2 April 1918 at 1530hrs the picket boat *Vorwärts* came alongside and the troops intended to occupy Russarö and Hango on the Finnish coast transferred to her. At the same time the first ice was sighted and later more ice fields of drifting ice. Early on the morning of 3 April at 0340hrs the church and water towers of Hango were sighted and at 0400hrs the order "Clear ship for battle" was given. Under the coast was thick drifting ice. At 0512hrs minesweepers signalled that Russarö was unoccupied and a short time later two explosions were observed ashore, then after a third explosion debris was seen falling on the ice. A large fire was seen on a ship in harbour. Further explosions and fires were seen ashore. At 0730hrs Shock Troops landed in Hango and from 0800hrs the transport fleet began running into harbour. *Posen* anchored off the mole, amongst drifting ice. On 5 April *Posen* coaled from the collier *Helene Hugo Stinnes* in weather that was partly foggy. On 9 April *Posen* was made flagship of the senior commander as *Westfalen* departed for Reval. Two days later *Posen* was instructed to go to Reval. Therefore that same day, 11 April 1918, the advance to Reval was undertaken through drifting ice on the open sea. From 1200 noon until 1530hrs *Posen* waited in thin ice off Reval and then began the advance to Helsingfors through more drifting ice. At 1800hrs a Russian warship, apparently *Peter Veliki*, with two merchant ships was sighted south of Helsingfors with course for Kronstadt. The Russians dipped their colours. At 1930hrs that evening *Posen* anchored off Grahara Island with *Westfalen*.

The following morning, 12 April, there was thick fog so that the battleships had to remain at anchor. During the afternoon the sounds of battle could be heard and as at 1710hrs the weather cleared *Posen* weighed anchor and resumed the advance. East of Grahara was a sunken steamer, near the sinking position of the English submarines. At 1840hrs *Posen* anchored off Sveaborg. *Grüß Gott* came alongside and took aboard the Landing Korps of *Posen*. During the evening and night the sounds of rifle and machine-gun fire could be heard ashore. *Posen's* Landing Korps were in combat until 1500hrs the following afternoon. That day, 13 April, *Posen* received orders to move to Langhörn Sound. That afternoon *Grüß Gott* and minesweeper *M88* had to intervene in the land battle with their artillery and only then were the Bolsheviks forced to negotiate a surrender.

On 14 April only sporadic rifle and machine-gun fire was heard and the Finnish authorities insisted

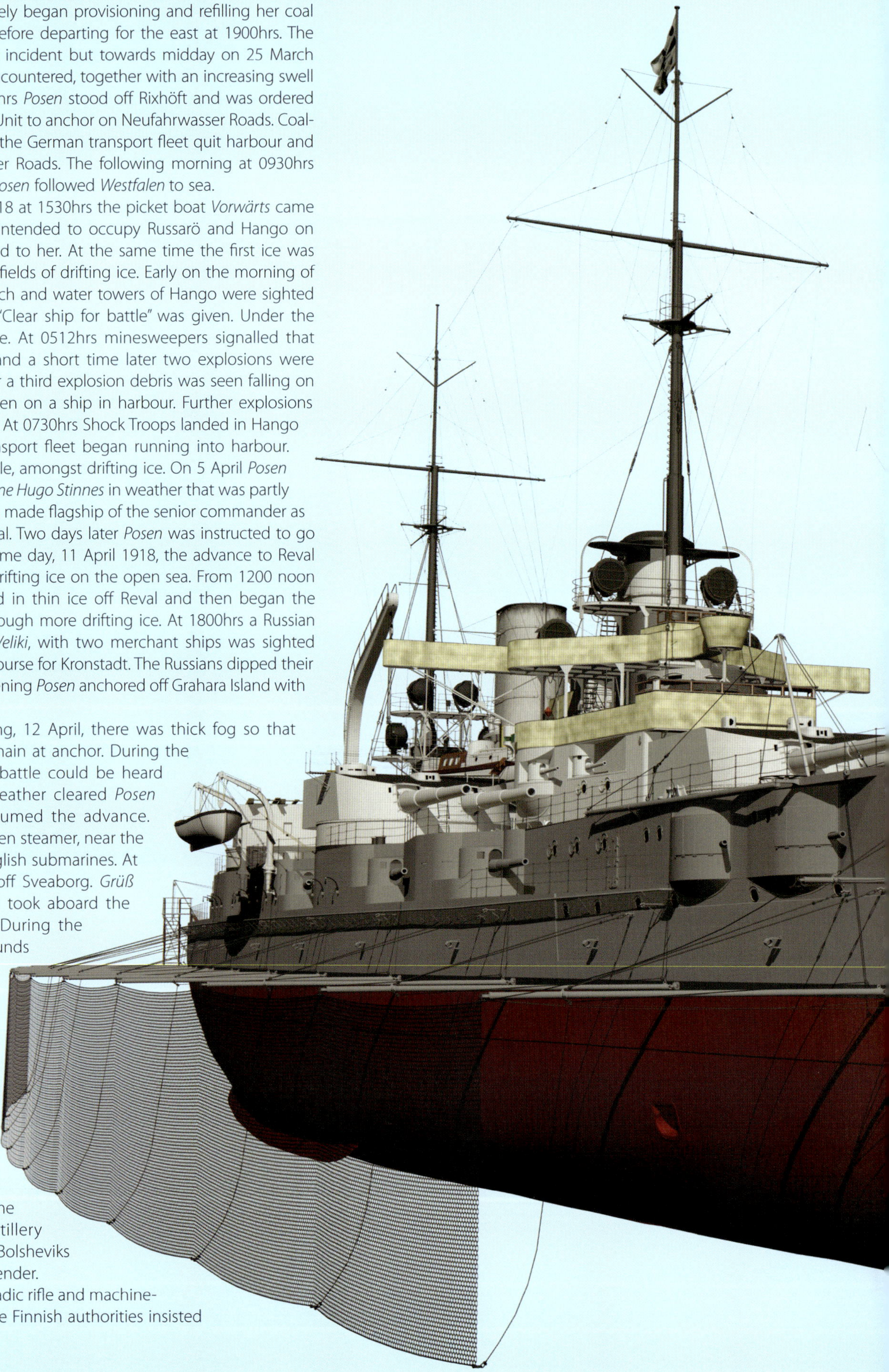

on a parade, despite German objections. As the participants gathered Red Guards opened fire on them so that the delegations from the ships had to duck for cover. During the landing operations the Landing Korps of *Posen* suffered four dead and 12 wounded, one badly.

Early on the morning of 16 April *Posen* began the trip to Reval, at first through pack ice and then in ice free waters, arriving at 0930hrs. Meanwhile, on 11 April at 0730hrs the battleship *Rheinland* had run aground on the rocks at Lagskär island. At 1800hrs *Posen* was ordered to go and render assistance. At 2255htrs on 17 April *Posen* anchored off Svenska Högarne, continuing the trip to Lagskär on 18 April and anchoring near the stranded battleship at 0855hrs. Nothing could be done to assist the grounded ship and at 0950hrs on 20 April *Posen* weighed anchor and began the return trip to Helsingfors. On 21 April *Posen* anchored off Russarö in thick fog, before later anchoring on Hango Roads, where she took coal from the collier *Orion*. On 22 April the journey to Helsingfors was continued however on anchoring off Helsingfors *Posen* pushed onto a wreck. Drivers revealed that the starboard and centre propellers were damaged and the ship required docking. *Posen* did not immediately go to Kiel, and only on 30 April at 1345hrs did she depart. At 1335hrs on 3 May *Posen* arrived in Kiel and went into Dock VII where work changing the propeller blades began the next day. On 9 May work was concluded and *Posen* began the canal trip back to the west, arriving on Wilhelmshaven Roads the following day.

On 16 May 1918 the I Squadron went into the North Sea a cover for minesweepers, returning the following morning. Another operation to cover minesweepers followed on 18–19 May and 27–29 May. On 18 June 1918 *Posen* and *Nassau* put to sea to cover minesweepers of the 8 MSHF working on Route 642. The 16 TBHF and three cruisers of the II AG also provided support. That night at 2330hrs, whilst on the return trip, an escorting torpedoboot, *V79*, reported a torpedo rack to starboard. *Posen* gave five short blasts on her horn and immediately turned away 8 points to port. *Nassau* also reported the torpedo track and *V79* dropped two depth charges. The journey was continued along Route Red and at 0628hrs on 19 June *Posen* anchored on Wilhelmshaven Roads.

On 21 June *Posen* ran into Wilhelmshaven and then into Dock V for replacement of the wooden bearings of all three propellers. This work continued until 9 July when *Posen* returned to Wilhelmshaven Roads. Early on the morning of 11 August 1918 six British motorboats were escorted into the southern North Sea by cruisers to mount an attack into the German Bight. *Posen* moved from Wilhelmshaven onto Schillig Roads and at 1615hrs raised anchor and ran out with *Westfalen*, with orders to join with the IV Squadron, consisting of *Kaiser* and *Kaiserin*. Nevertheless, because of mechanical problems *Kaiserin* remained in the Jade. The Unit steered into the North Sea on Route Green. Many drifting mines were seen. At 0130hrs on 12 August a turn was made back to Schillig Roads without there being any enemy contact. At 1545hrs that afternoon *Posen* put to sea on Route 600 and went to the west for security of the III Mine Sweeper Flottille. At 2230hrs *Posen* anchored near Point F.

At 0530hrs on 13 August anchor was weighed and *Posen* steered to the west together with *Markgraf* and *Kronprinz Wilhelm*. During the day the minesweeper *T67* ran onto a mine and sank whilst working on Route 642. At 2236hrs that night *Posen* anchored with *Markgraf* and *Kronprinz Wilhelm* in Square 2691 L, a little to the west of the previous nights anchorage on Route 300. The next morning at 0520hrs *Posen* weighed anchor and spent the day travelling up and down on Route 600, 700 and 750 before finally at 2000hrs beginning the return trip to the Jade. Only at 0500hrs on 15 August did *Posen* drop anchor on Schillig Roads, after being at sea for four consecutive days.

After five days in Wilhelmshaven *Posen* was at sea again supporting minesweepers on 25–26 August. On 5 September *Posen* again put to sea to support minesweeping but returned to Schillig Roads the same day. On 6 September Fleet evolutions were carried out before resuming picket duty. More Fleet evolutions followed on 24 September. Squadron training in the North Sea followed on 30 September and 2 October.

On 14 October at 0100hrs *Posen* and *Oldenburg* put to sea to cover the 9 MSHF with their work on Route 500. By 0830hrs *Posen* had reached Point 503. The 9 MSHF worked in Grid Squares K 137–187, covered by the IV AG consisting of *Regensburg*, *Straßburg* and *Nürnberg*. *Posen* ran up and down from Point 503 on Route 500, within sight of the cruisers. At 1925hrs *Posen* and *Oldenburg* anchored in Square 2834 L. On 15 October *Posen* and *Oldenburg* again stood up and down on Route 400 and 500, before again anchoring for the night in Square 2834 L. Early on the morning of 16 October *Posen* and *Oldenburg* weighed anchor and went along Route 500 towards Point 503, where they met the cruiser *Dresden* and the 9 MSHF. The minesweepers advised that minesweeping was impossible because of the weather, so therefore the battleships returned to Schillig Roads. After spending some time in Wilhelmshaven the I Squadron put to sea to cover minesweeping on Route Blue, anchoring overnight in Square 2341 L. The following day they returned to the Jade.

Posen stood ready to participate in the planned Fleet operation of 30 October 1918, however the operation was cancelled. On 3 November the I Squadron went to the Elbe river and on 9 November returned to Wilhelmshaven. On 16 December *Posen* was officially decommissioned.

Posen did not belong to the unit of interned ships, but was stricken from the list of warships on 5 November 1919 and was allocated to Britain on 13 May 1920. The British sold her to Holland for scrap and she was wrecked in 1922.

Close up orthographic views of the port side.

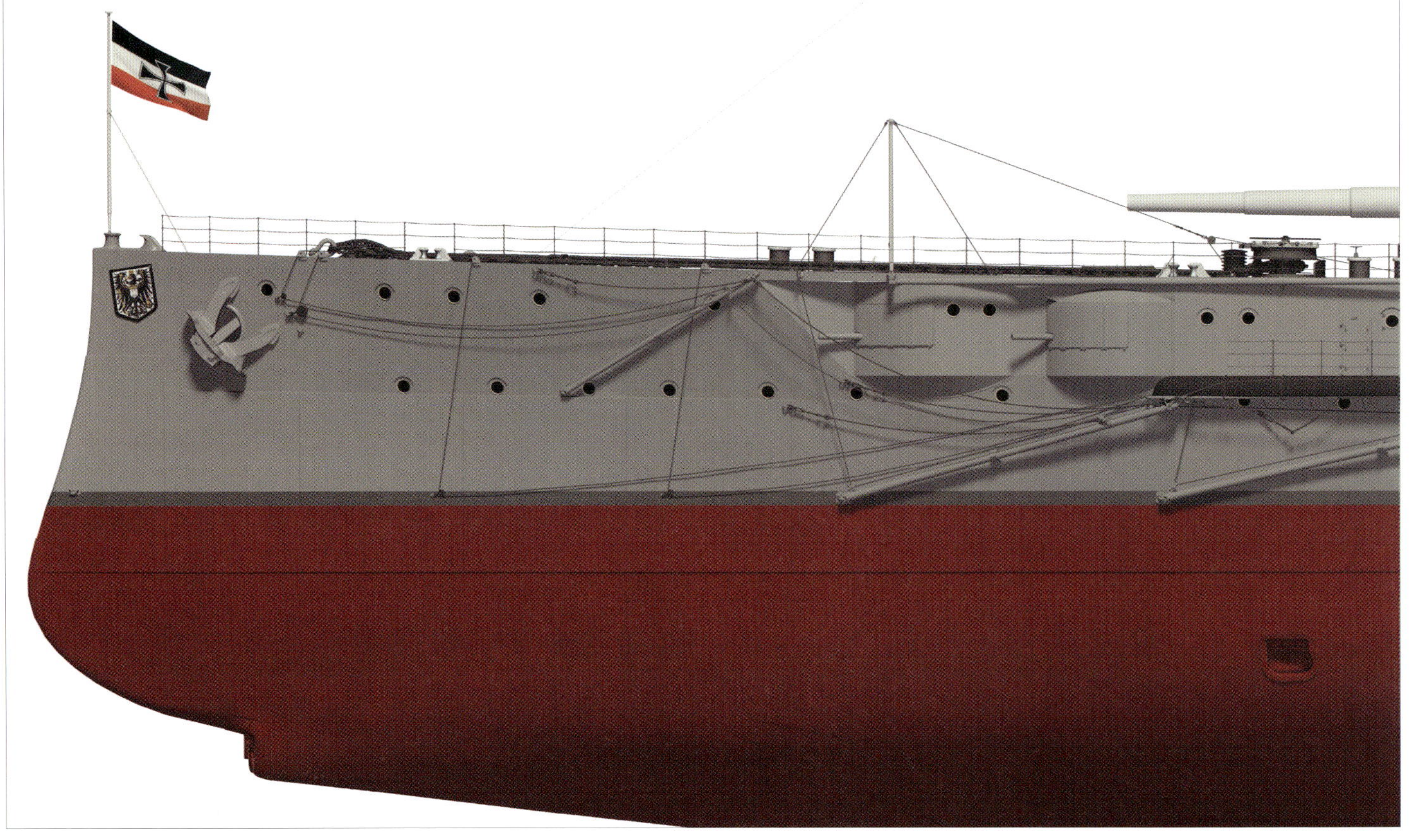

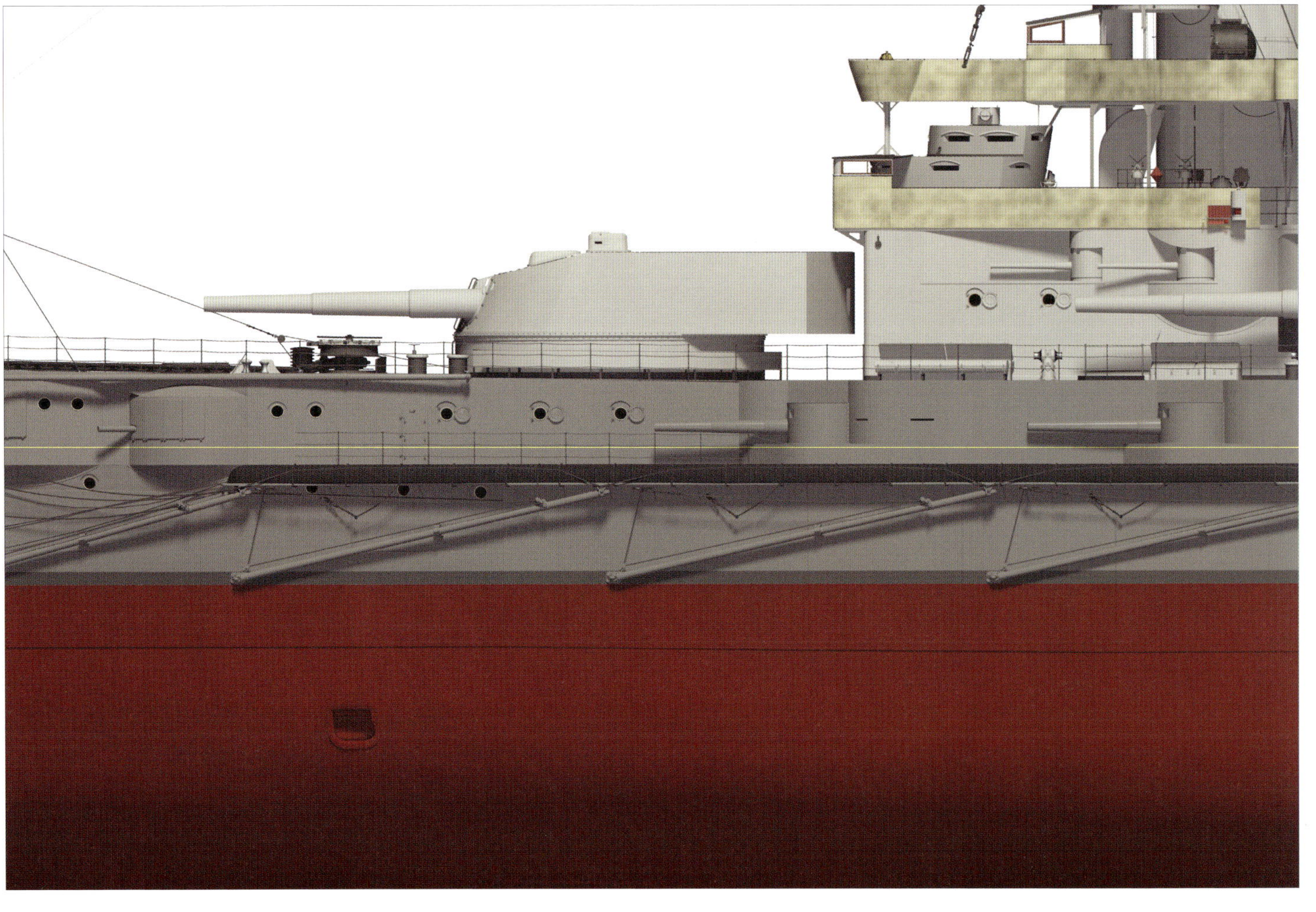

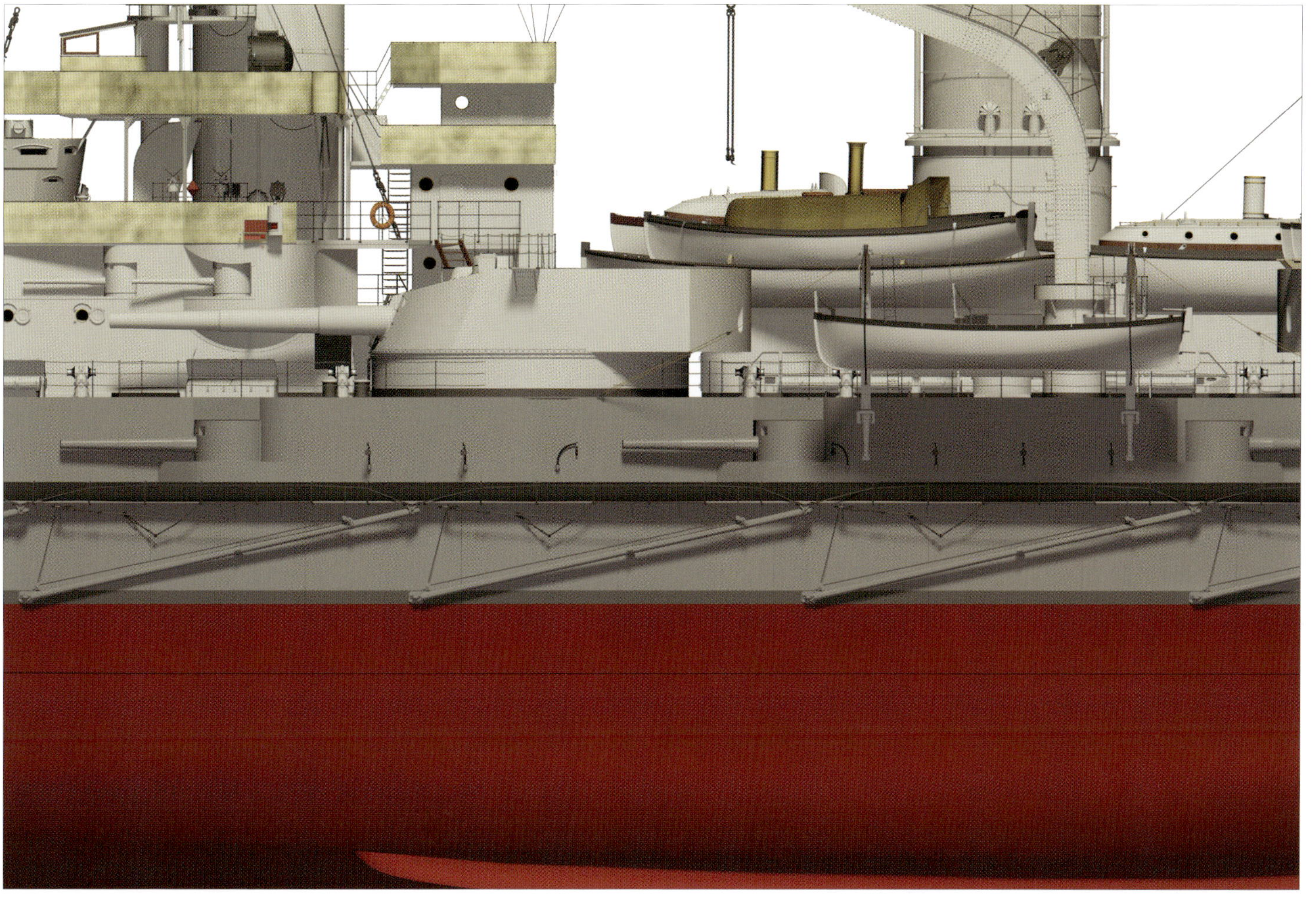

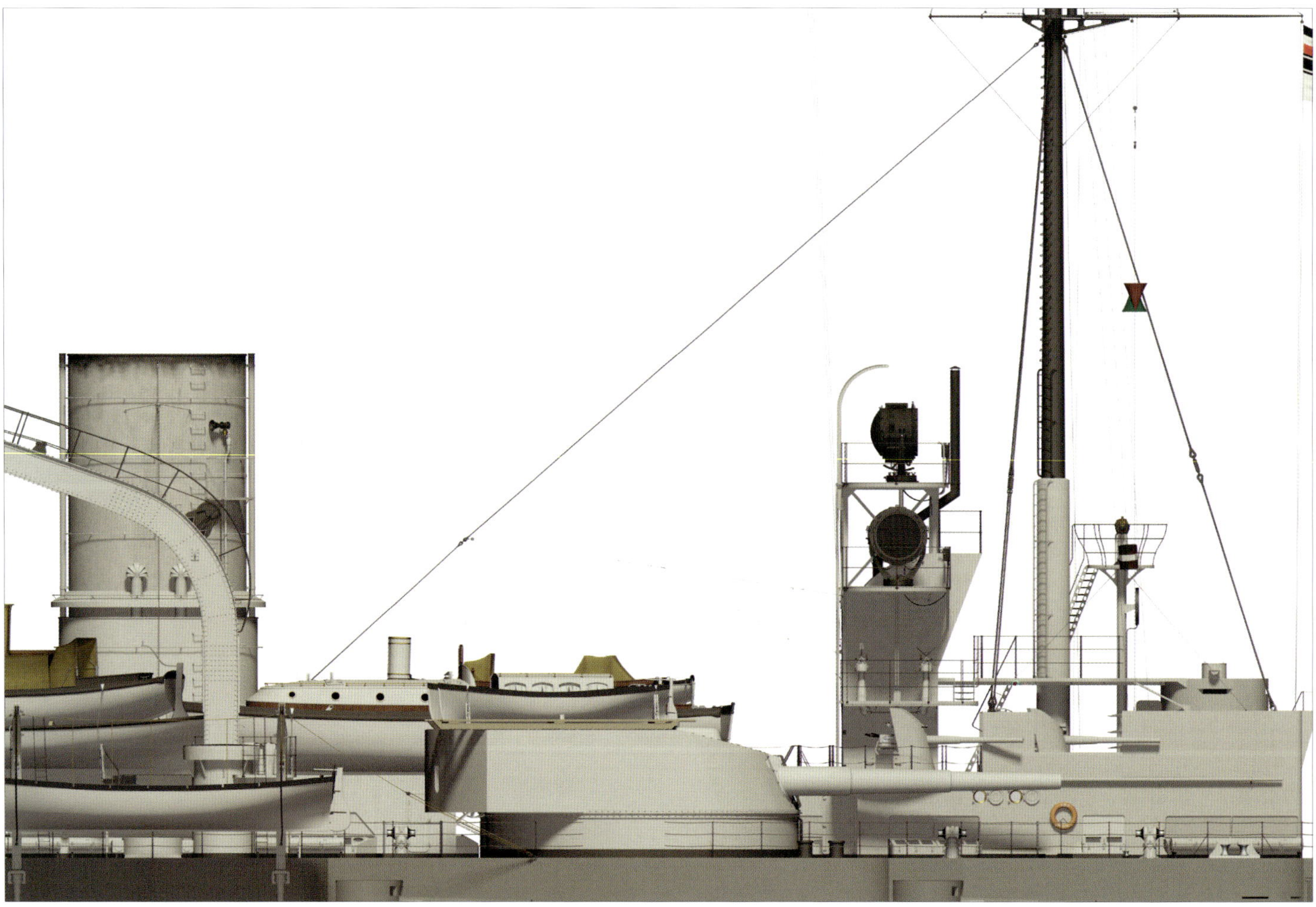

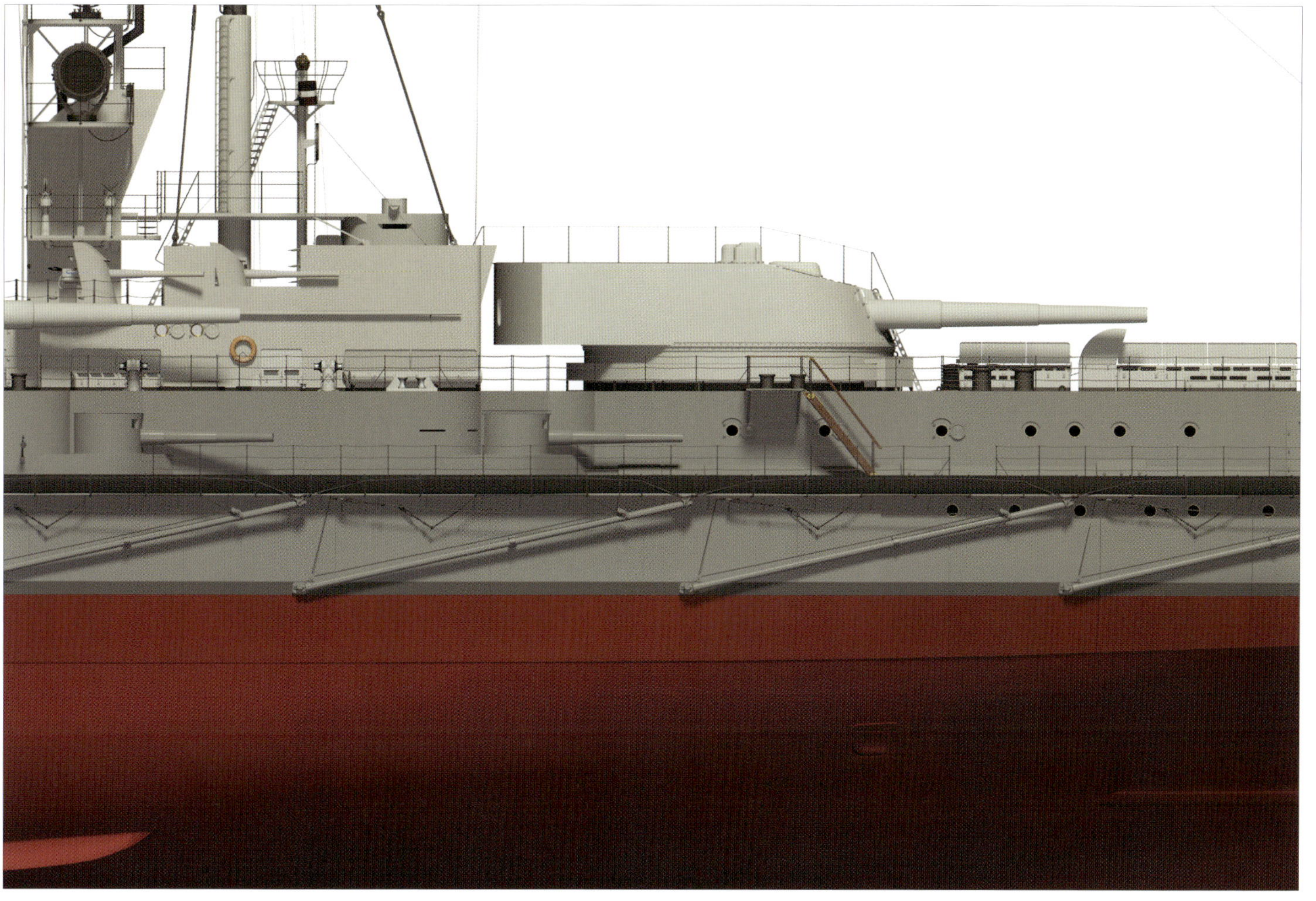

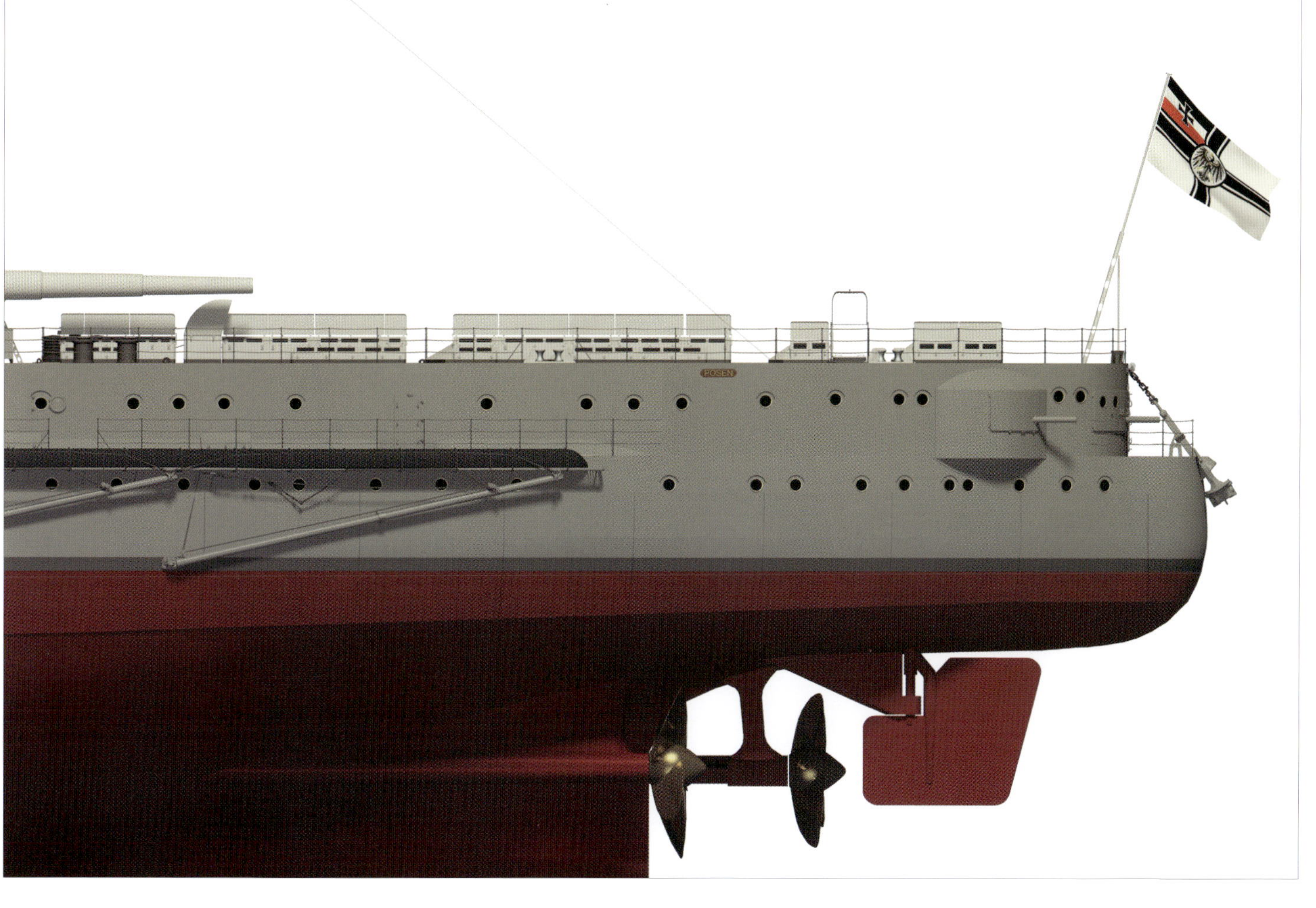

Close up orthographic views of the starboard side.

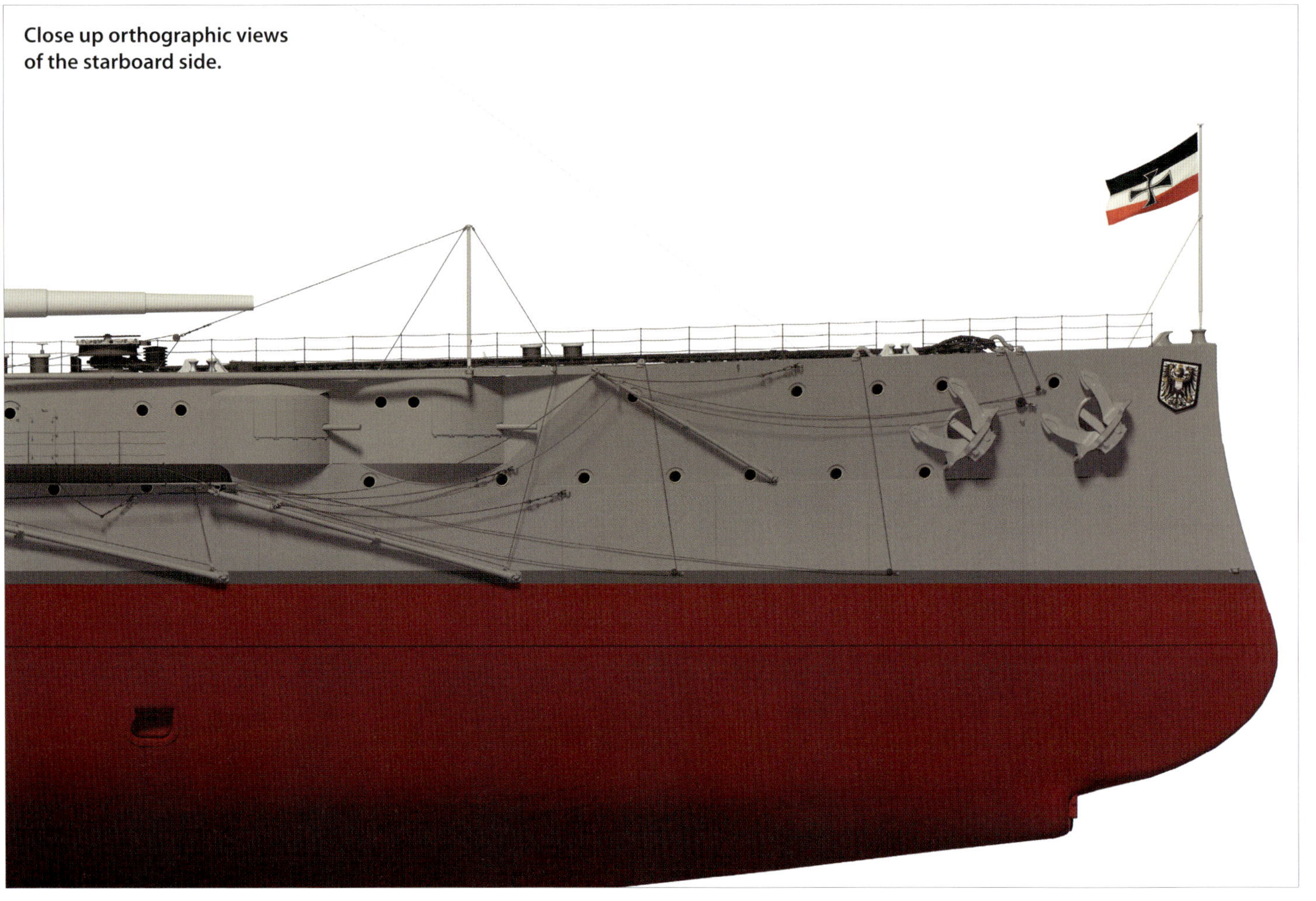

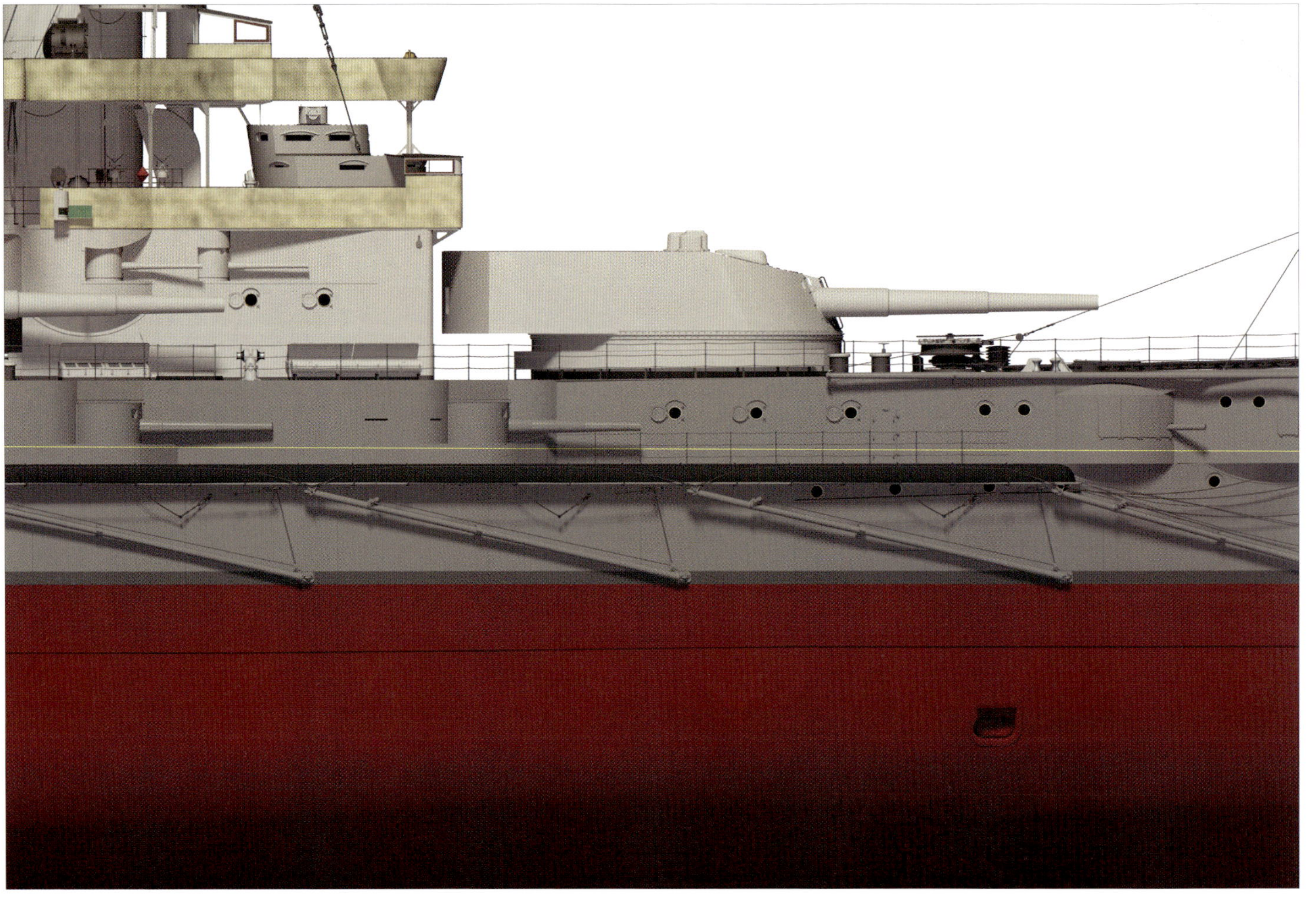

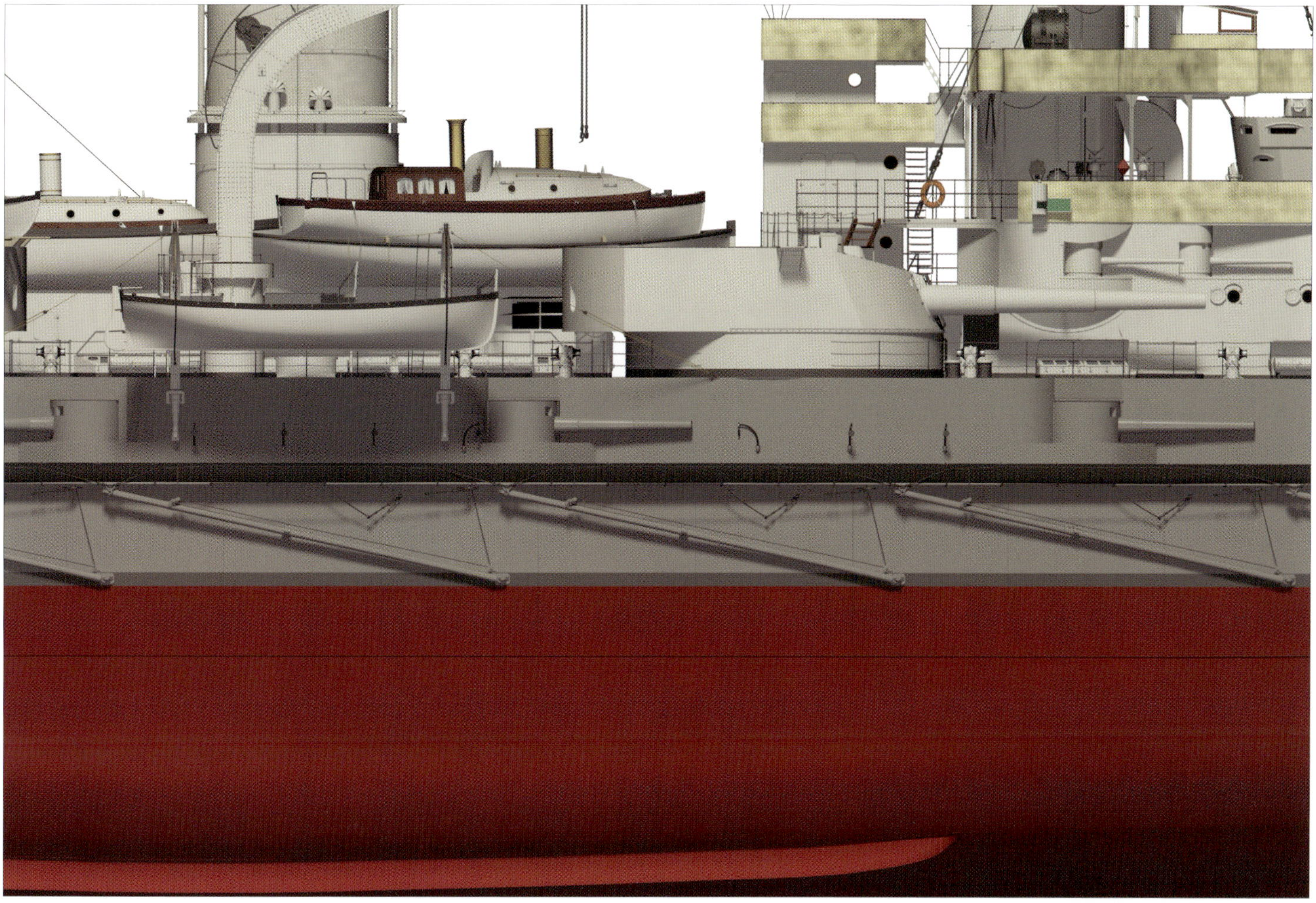

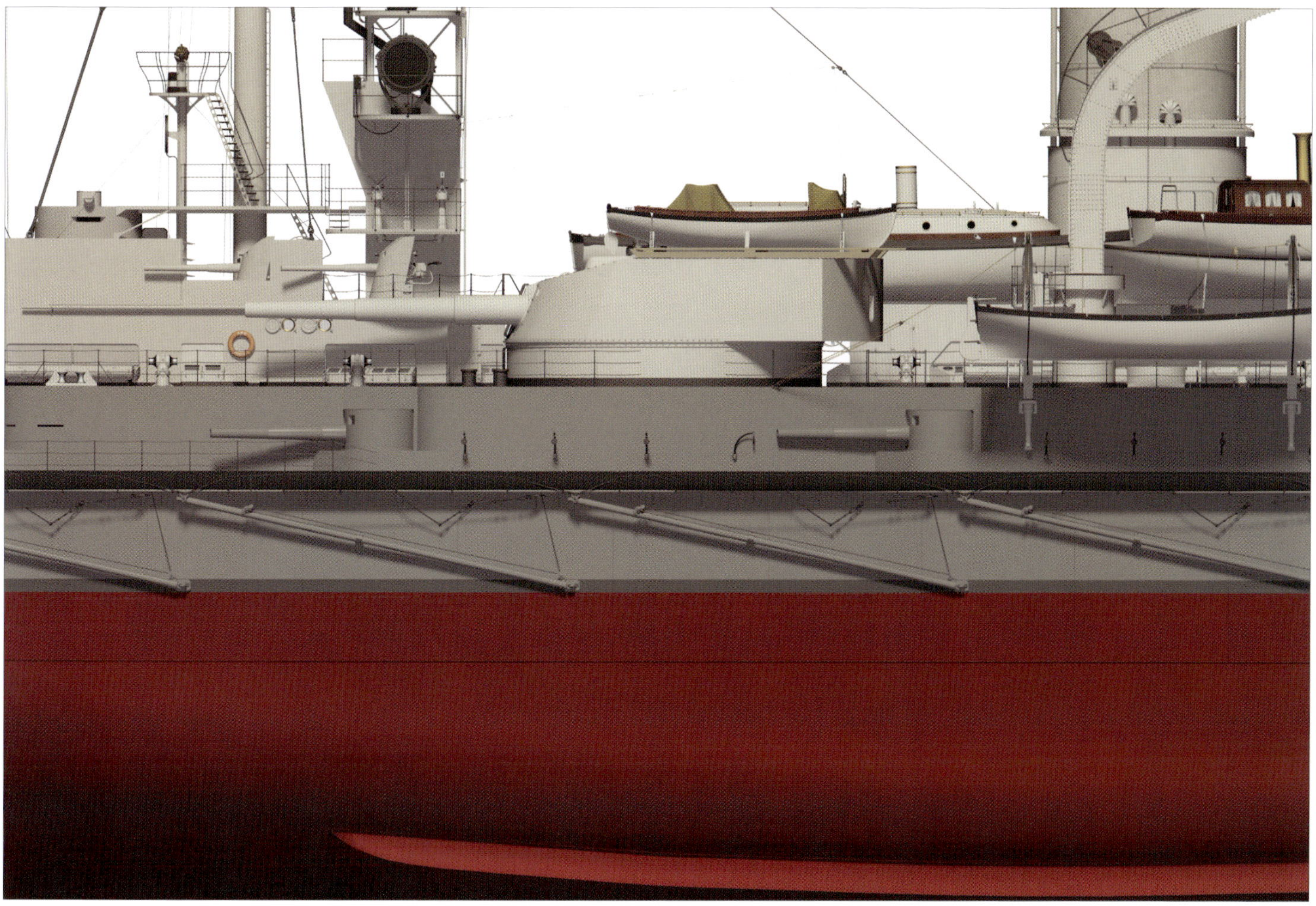

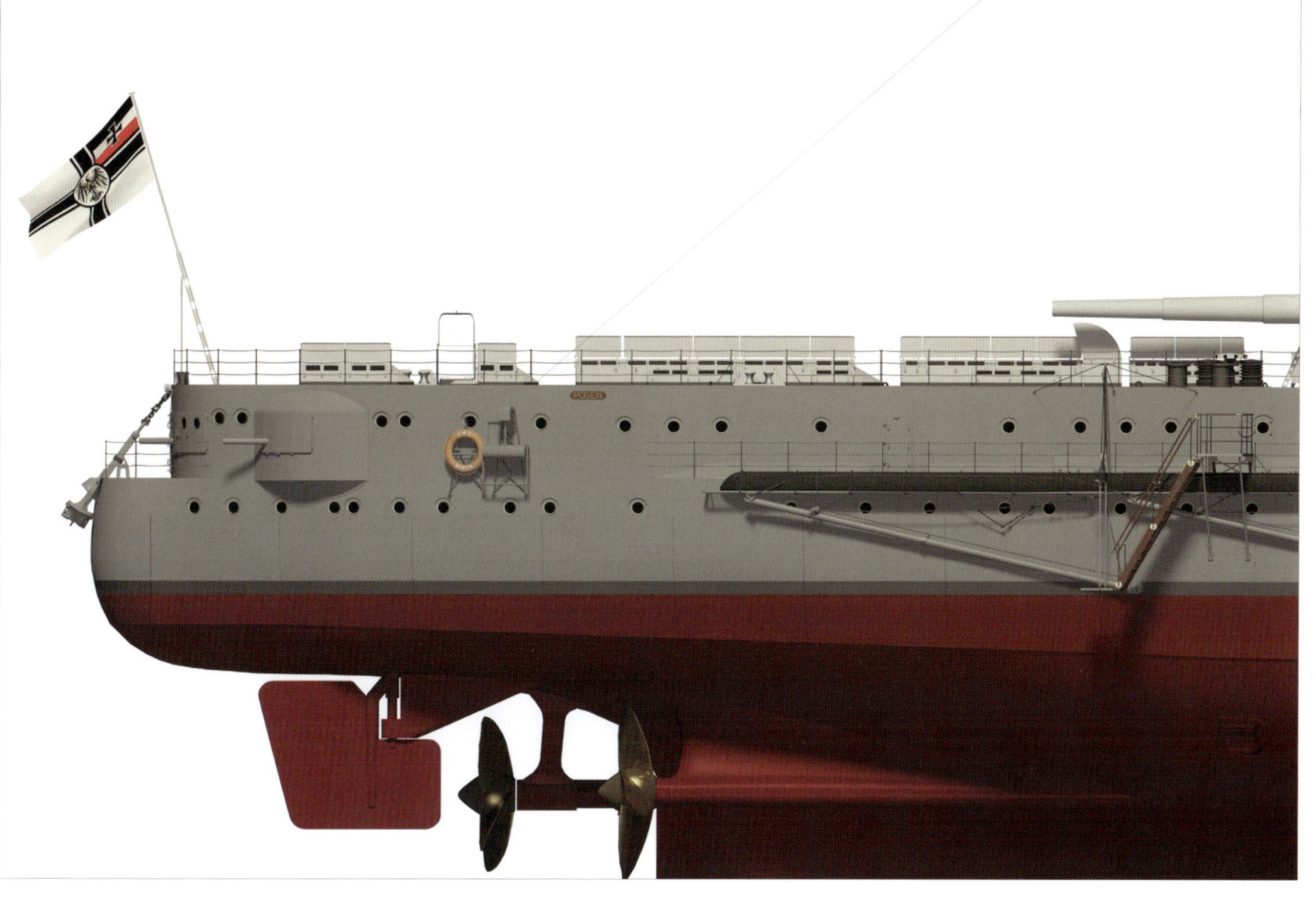

Orthographic top views.

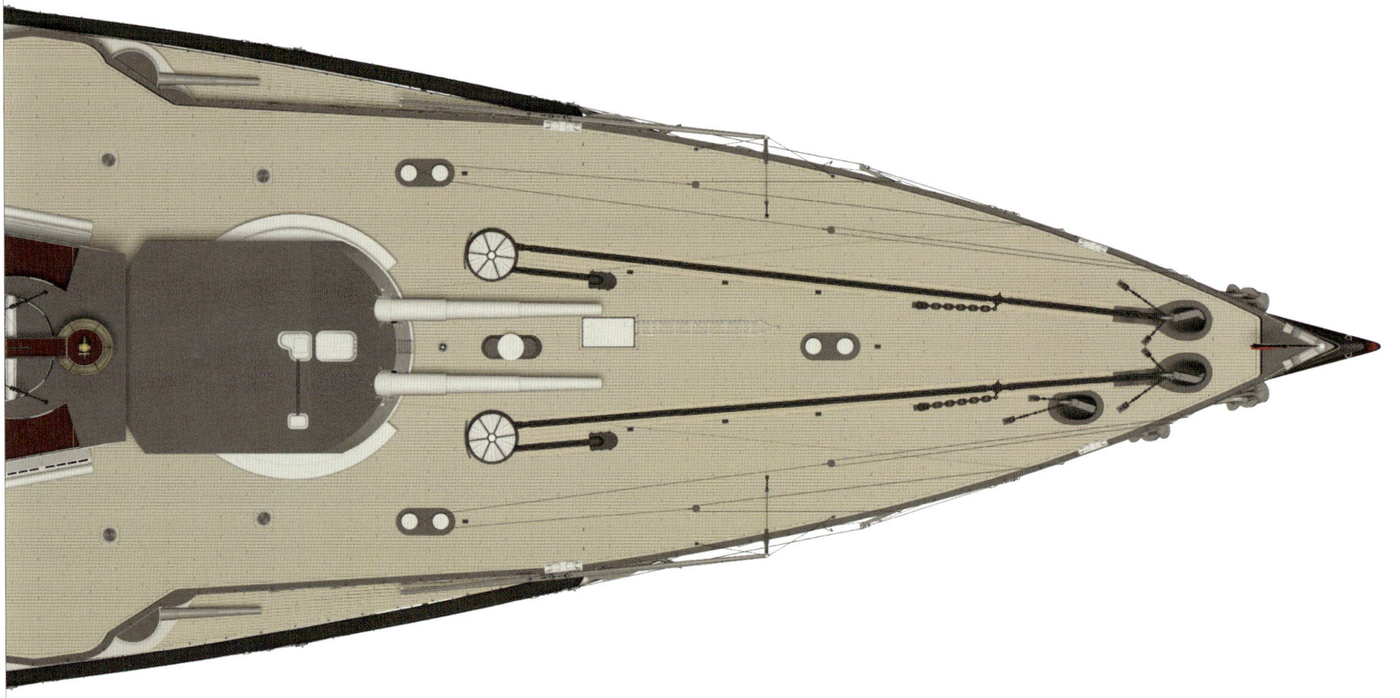

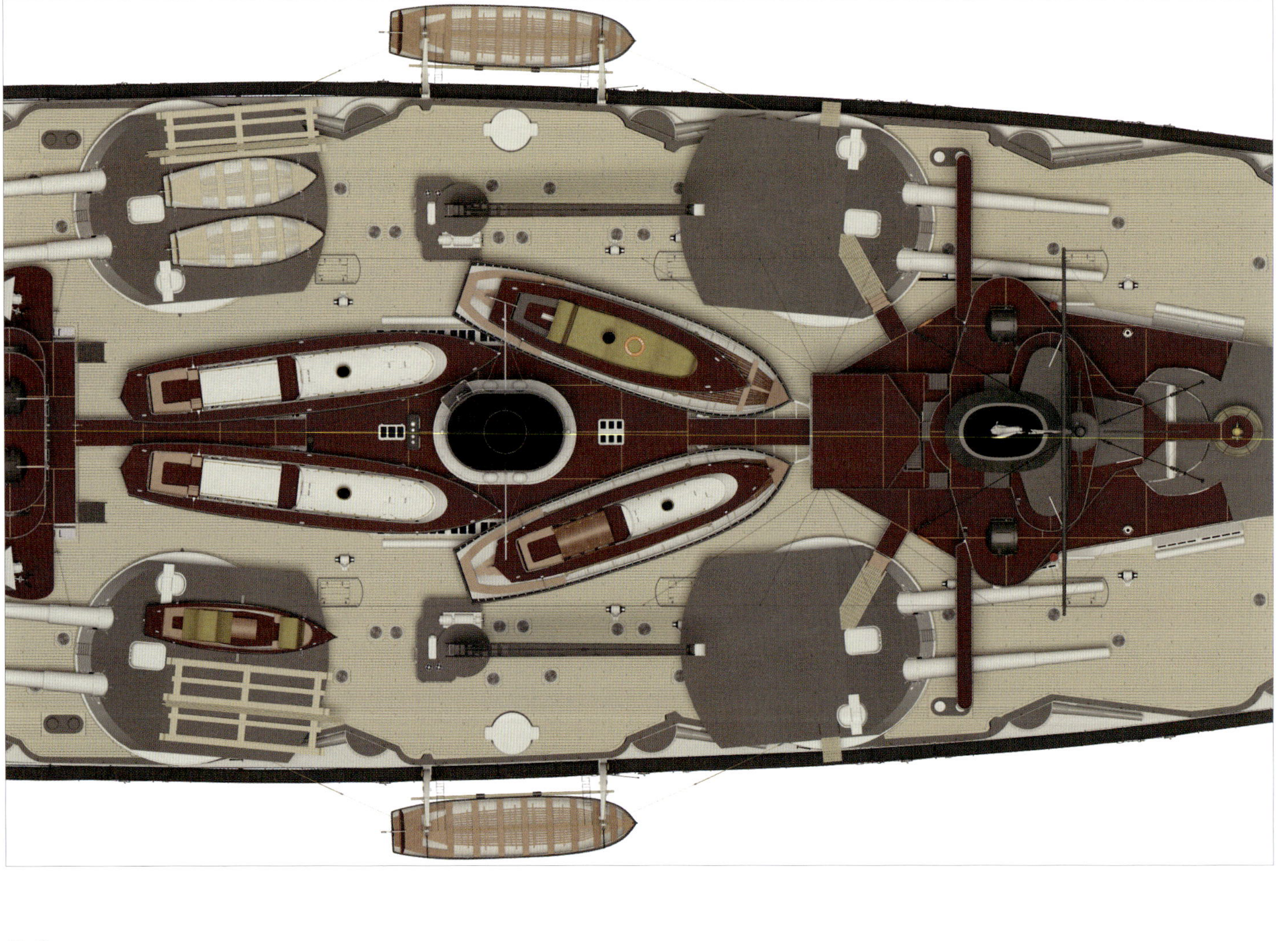

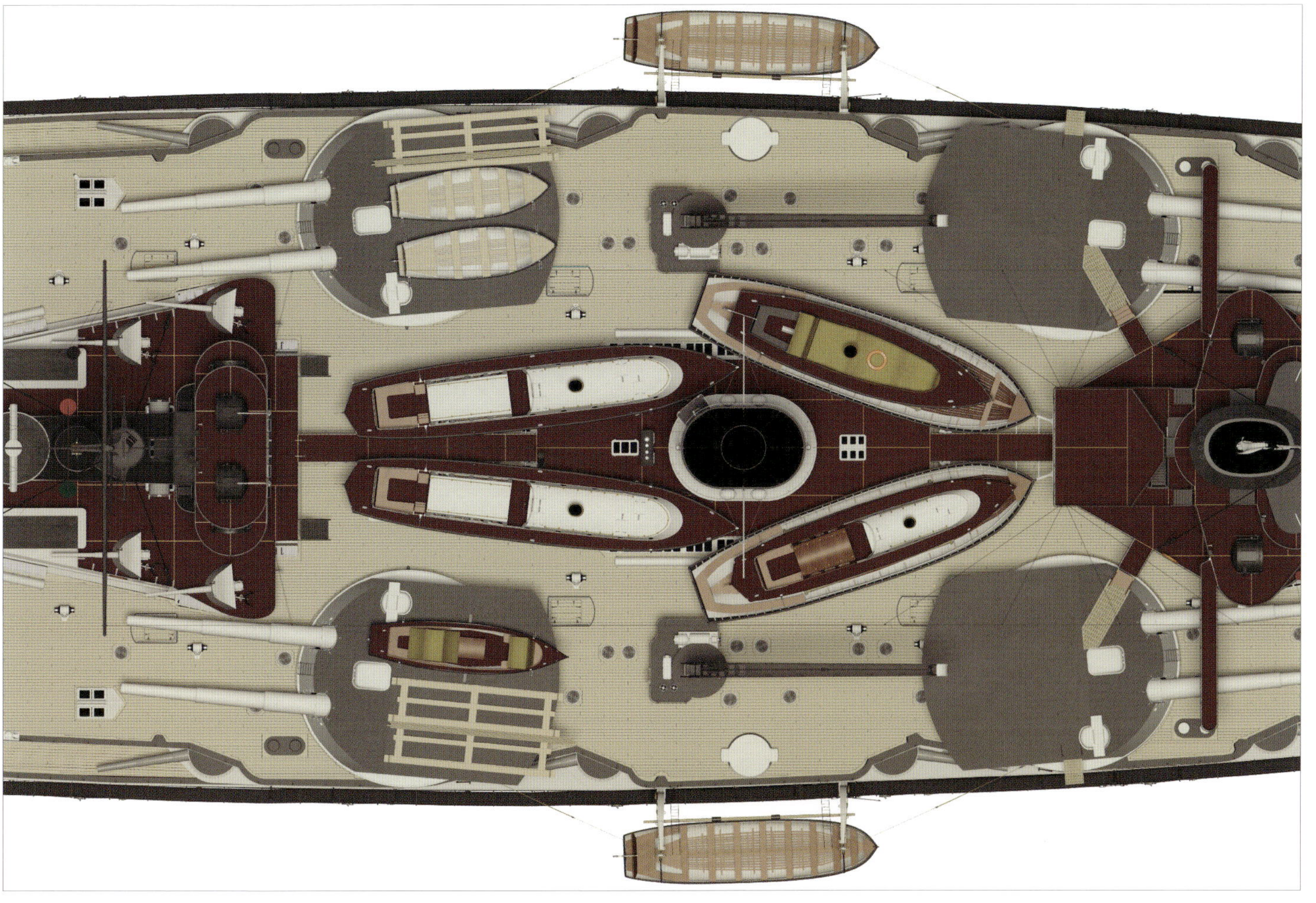

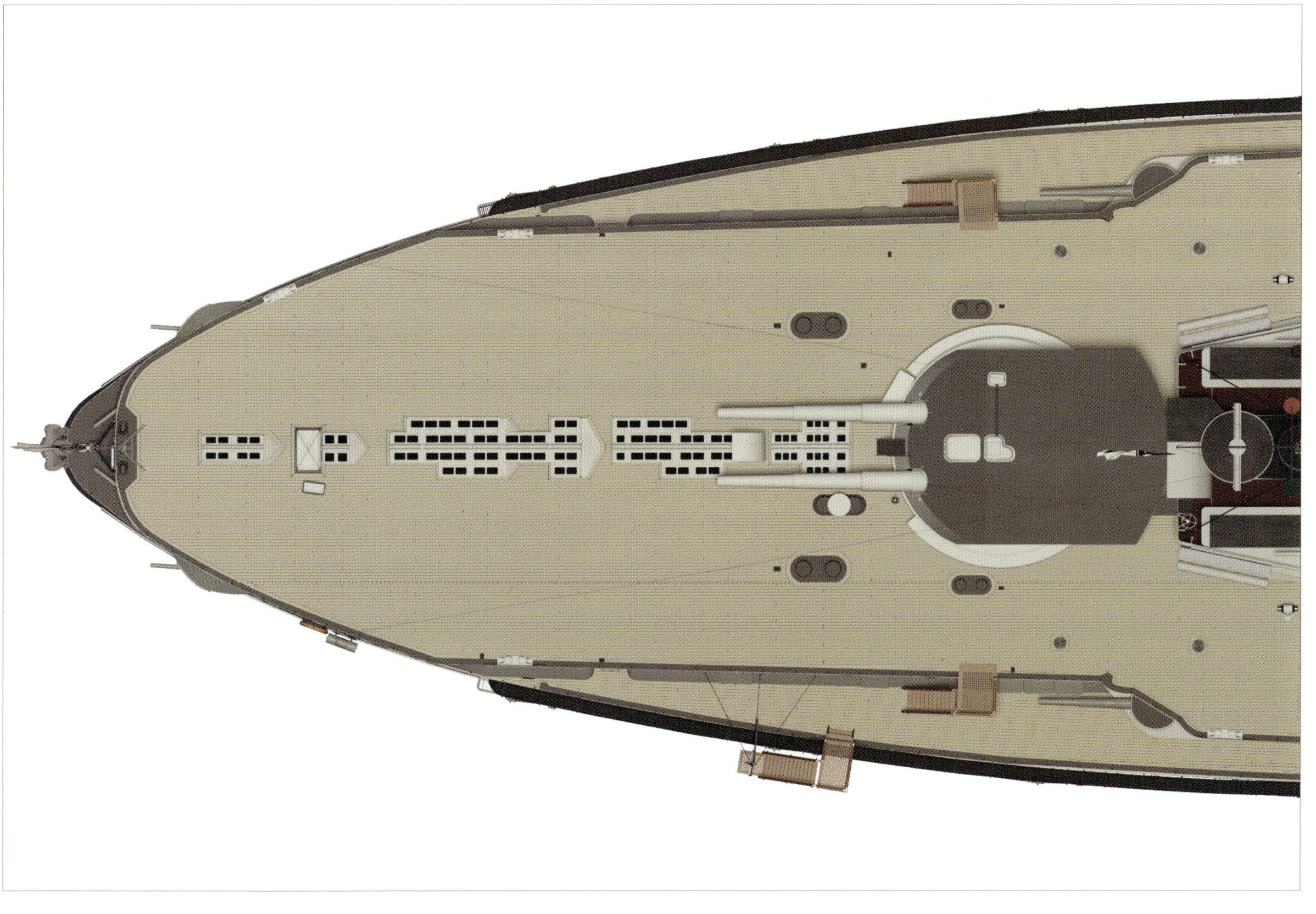

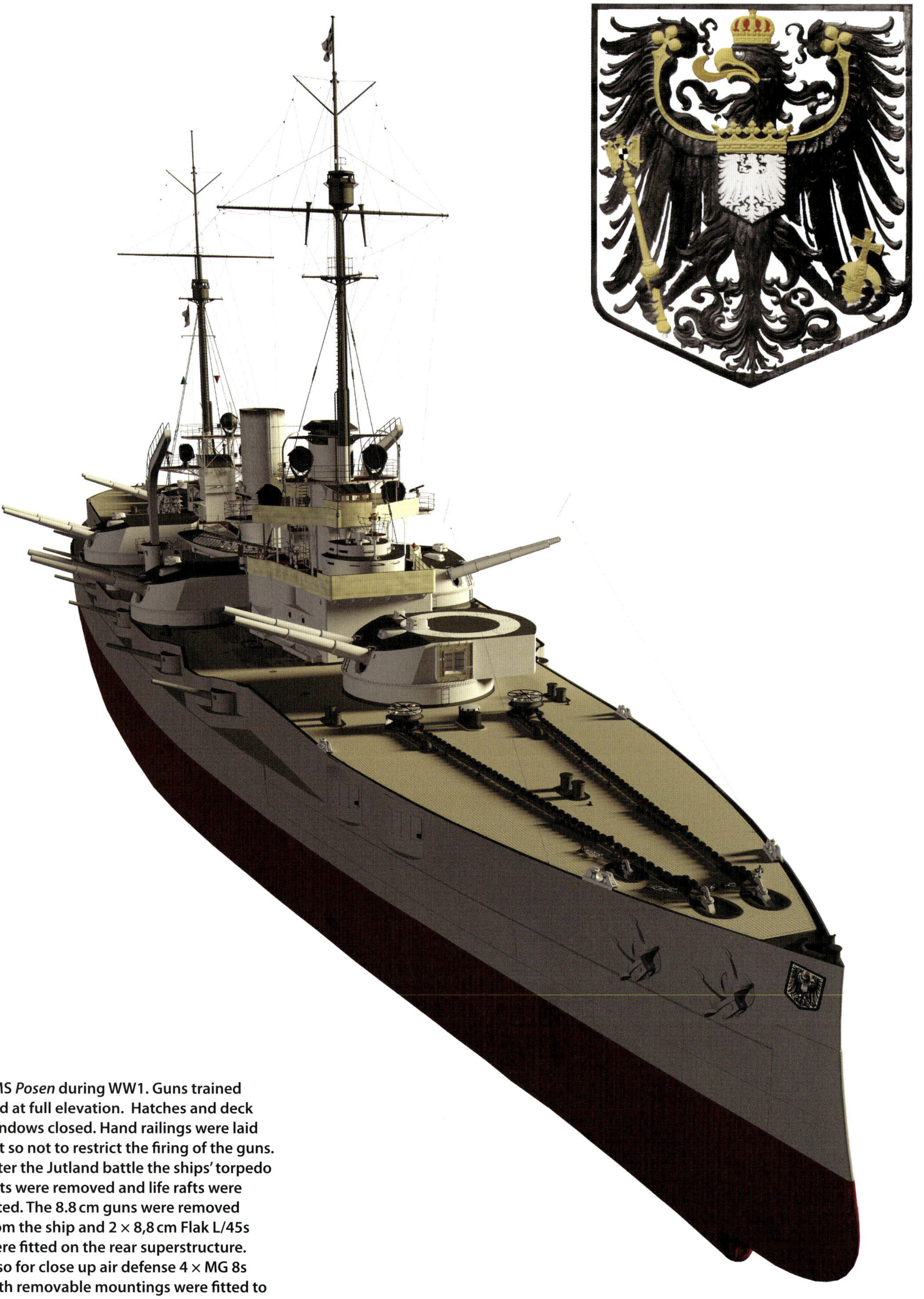

SMS *Posen* during WW1. Guns trained and at full elevation. Hatches and deck windows closed. Hand railings were laid flat so not to restrict the firing of the guns. After the Jutland battle the ships' torpedo nets were removed and life rafts were fitted. The 8.8 cm guns were removed from the ship and 2 × 8,8 cm Flak L/45s were fitted on the rear superstructure. Also for close up air defense 4 × MG 8s with removable mountings were fitted to extended lower searchlight platforms.

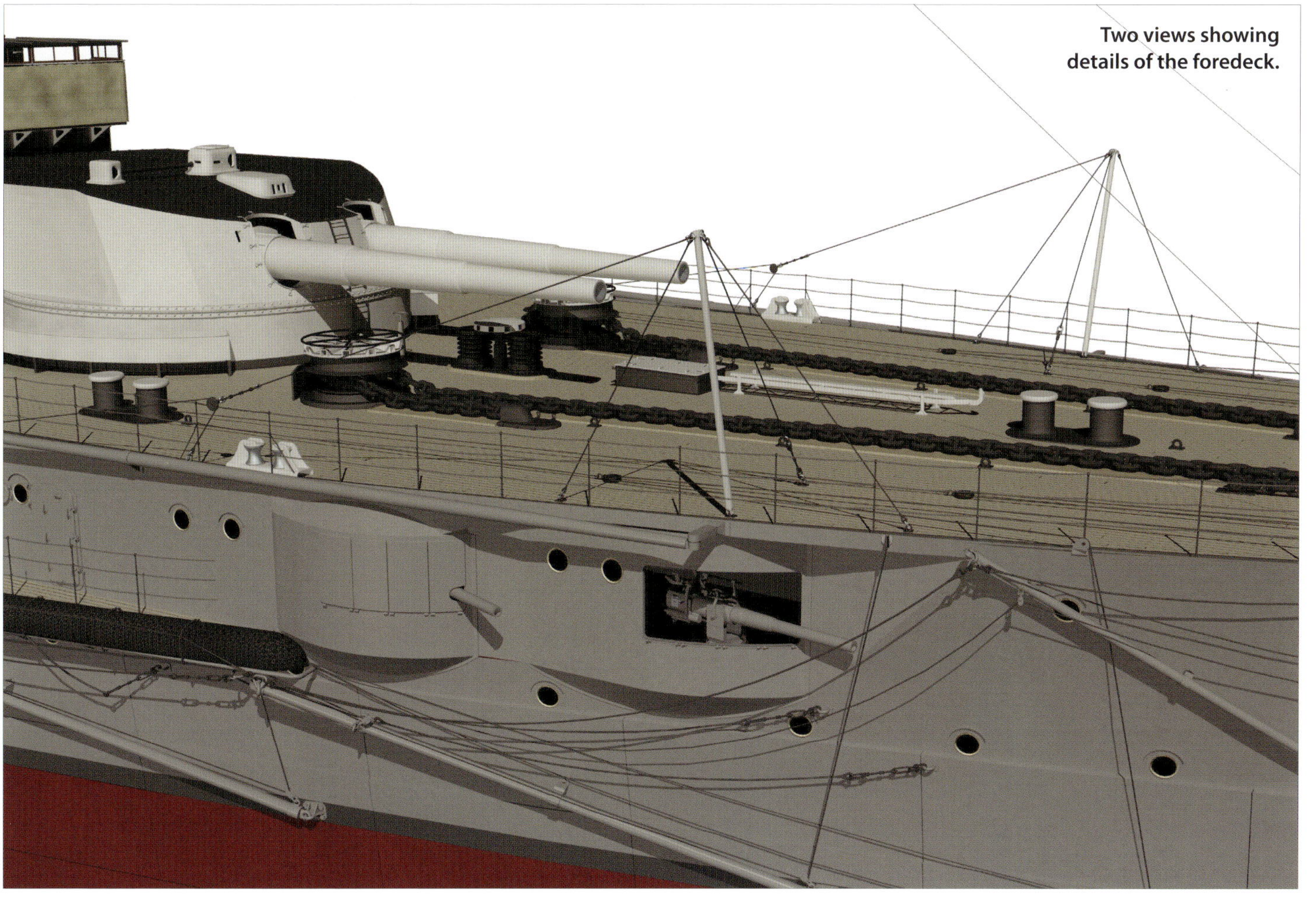

Two views showing details of the foredeck.

Two views of the starboard side of the bows including the forward and broadside firing torpedo tubes.

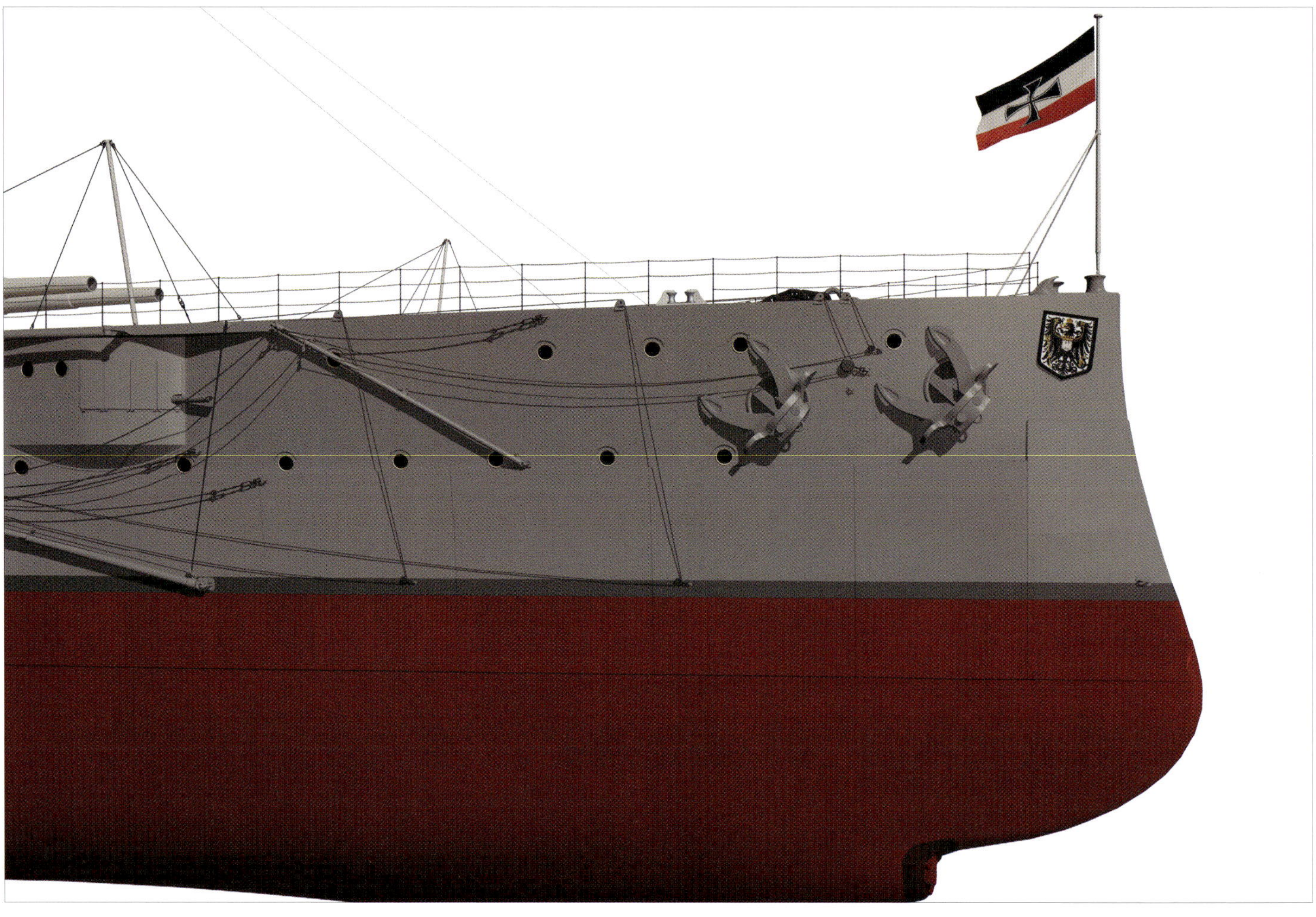

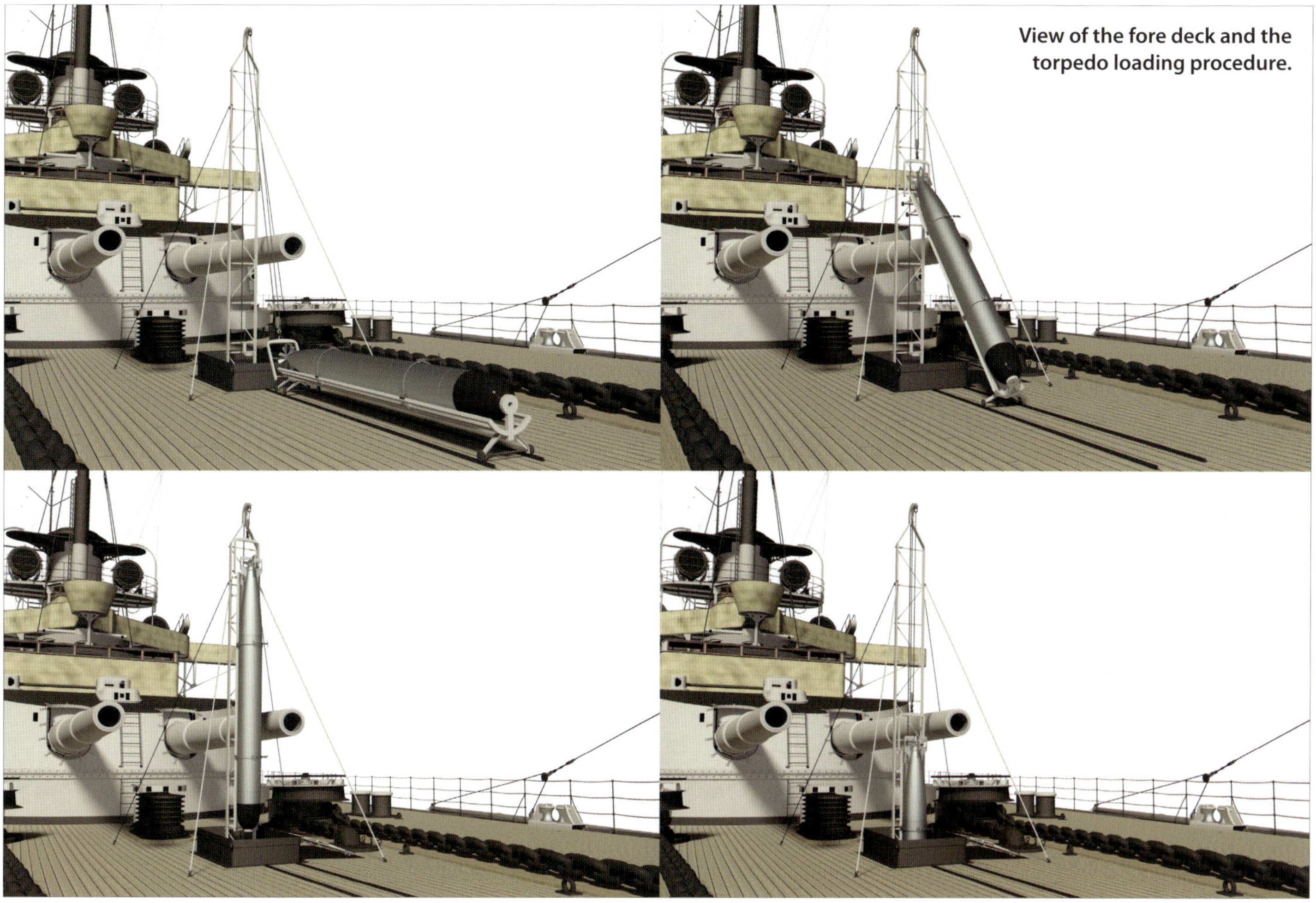

View of the fore deck and the torpedo loading procedure.

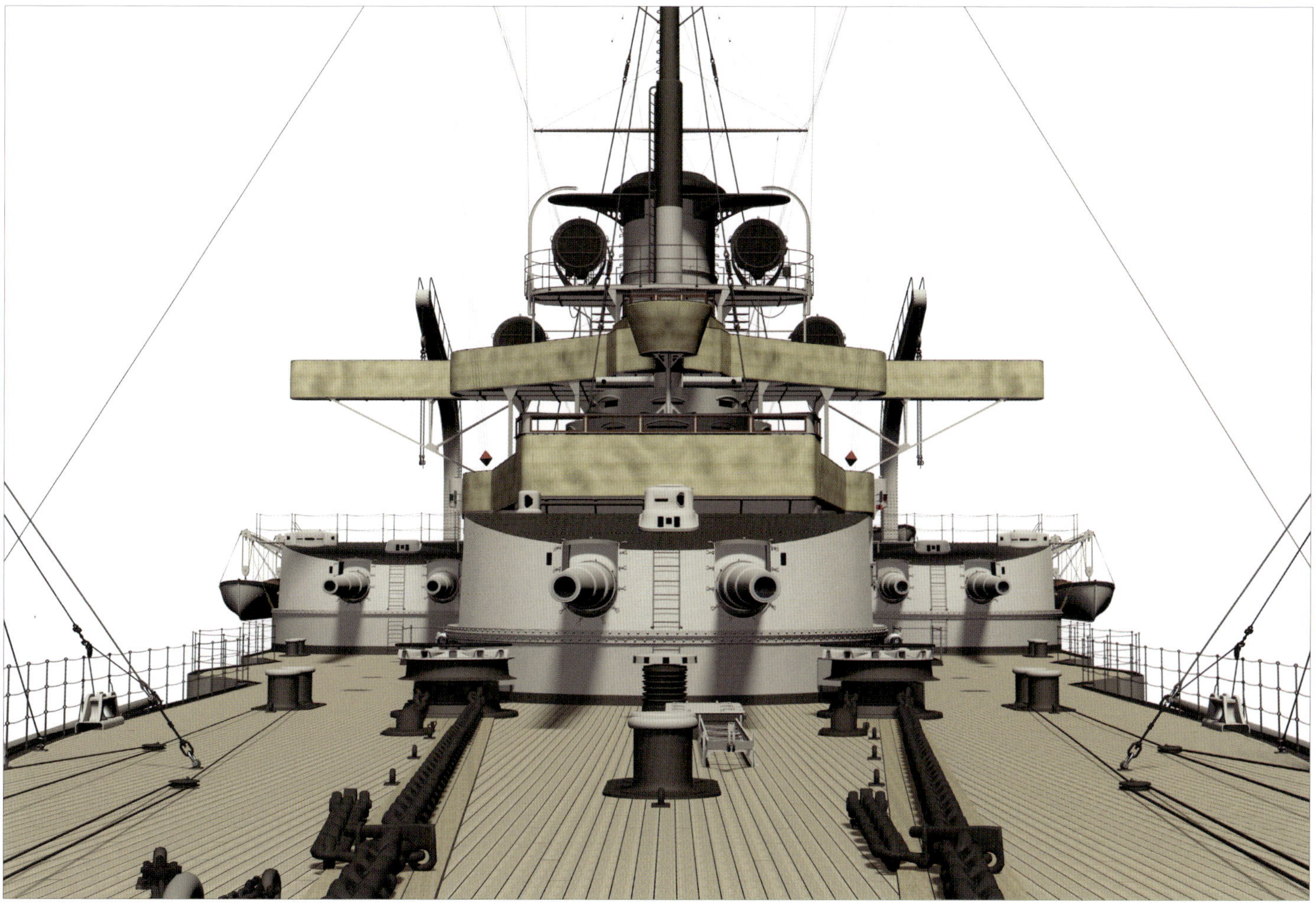

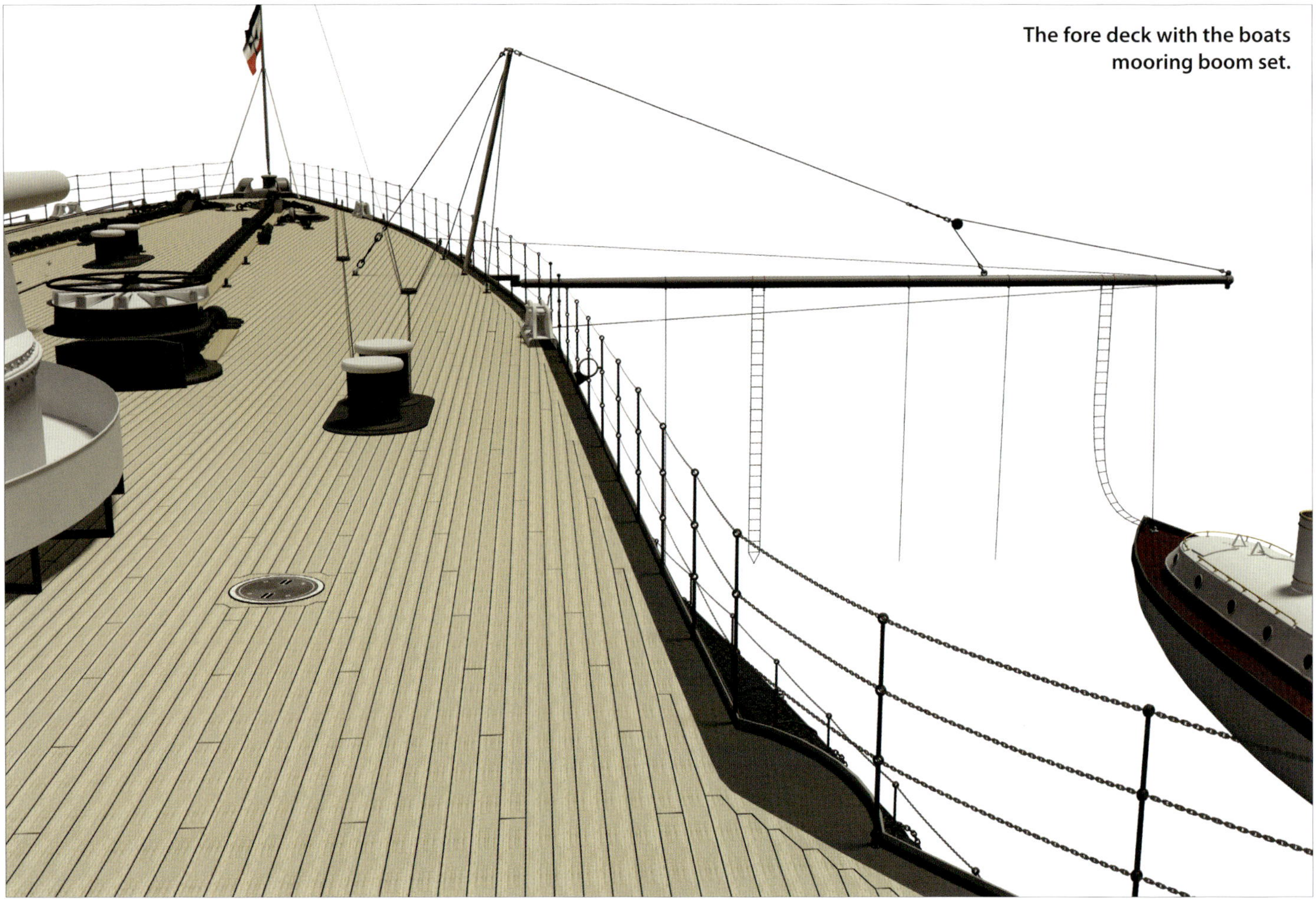

The fore deck with the boats mooring boom set.

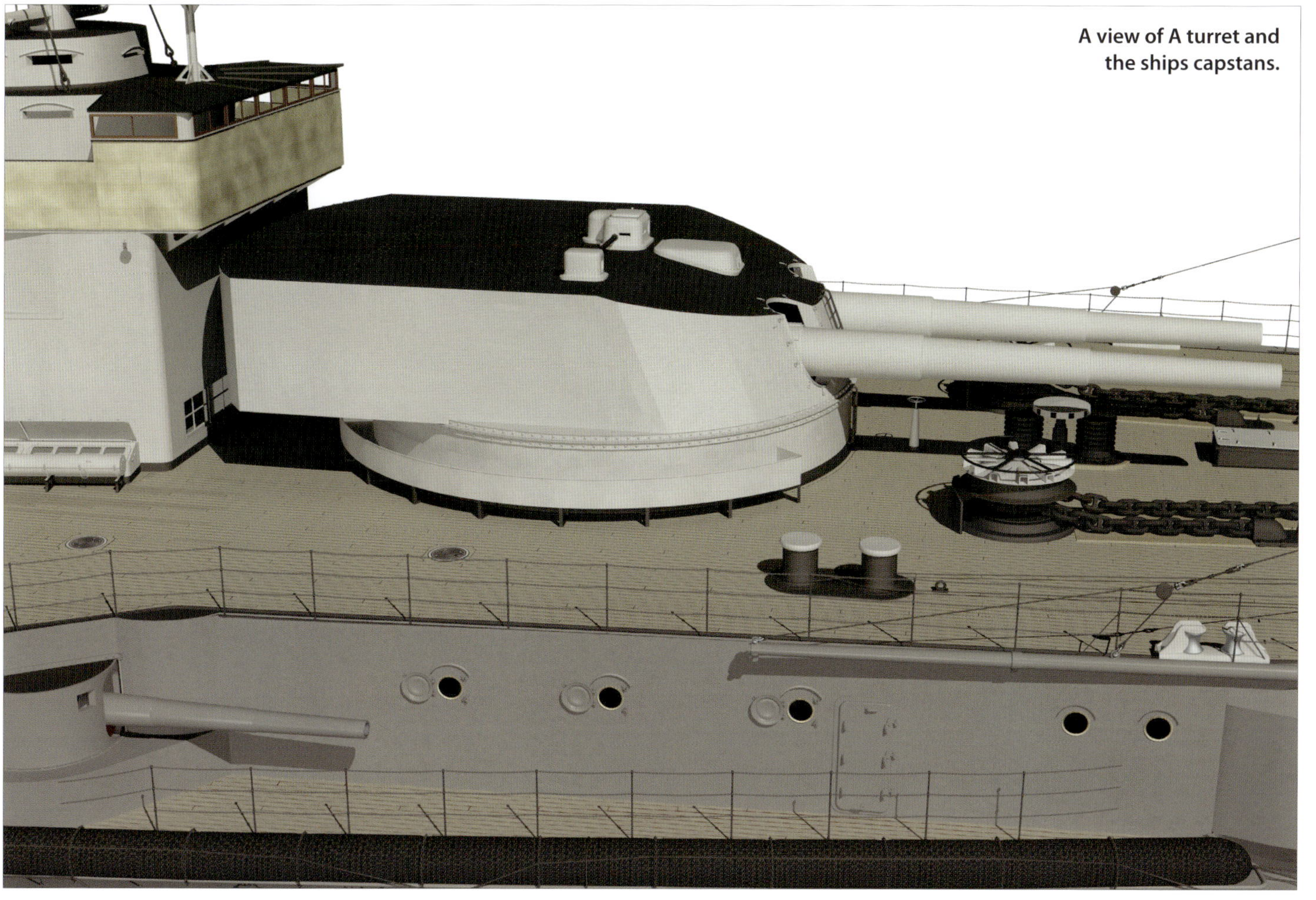

A view of A turret and the ships capstans.

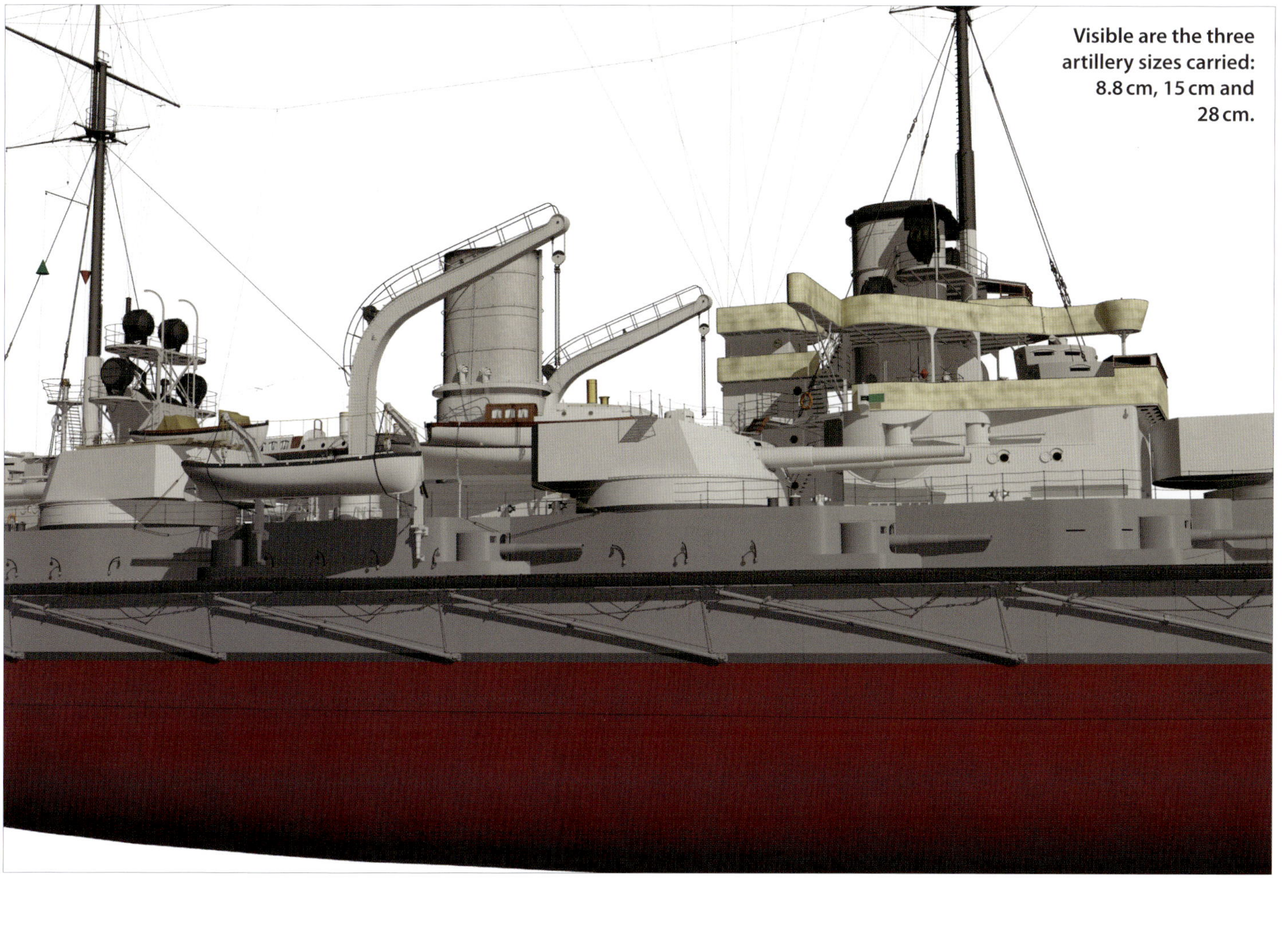

Visible are the three artillery sizes carried: 8.8 cm, 15 cm and 28 cm.

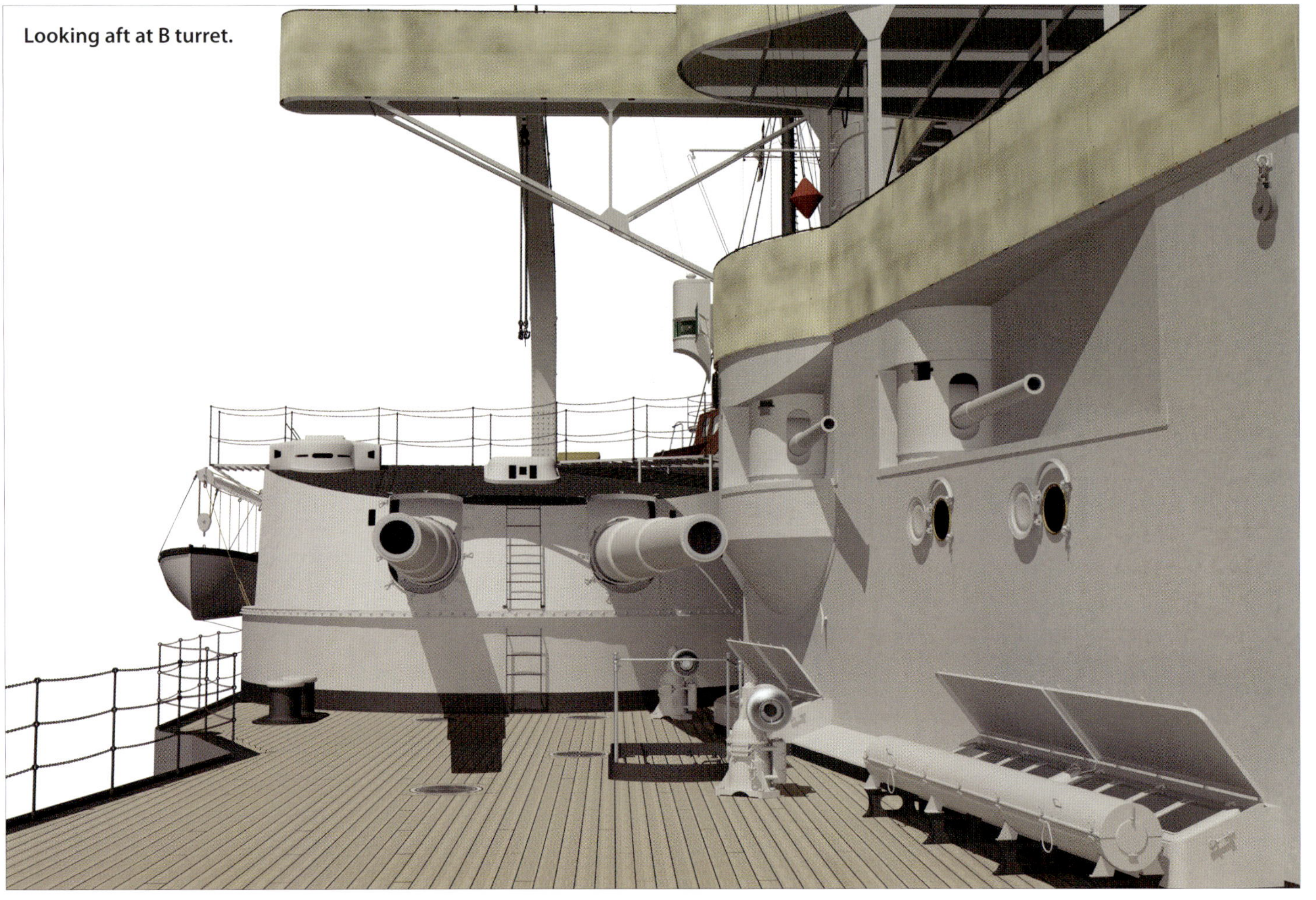
Looking aft at B turret.

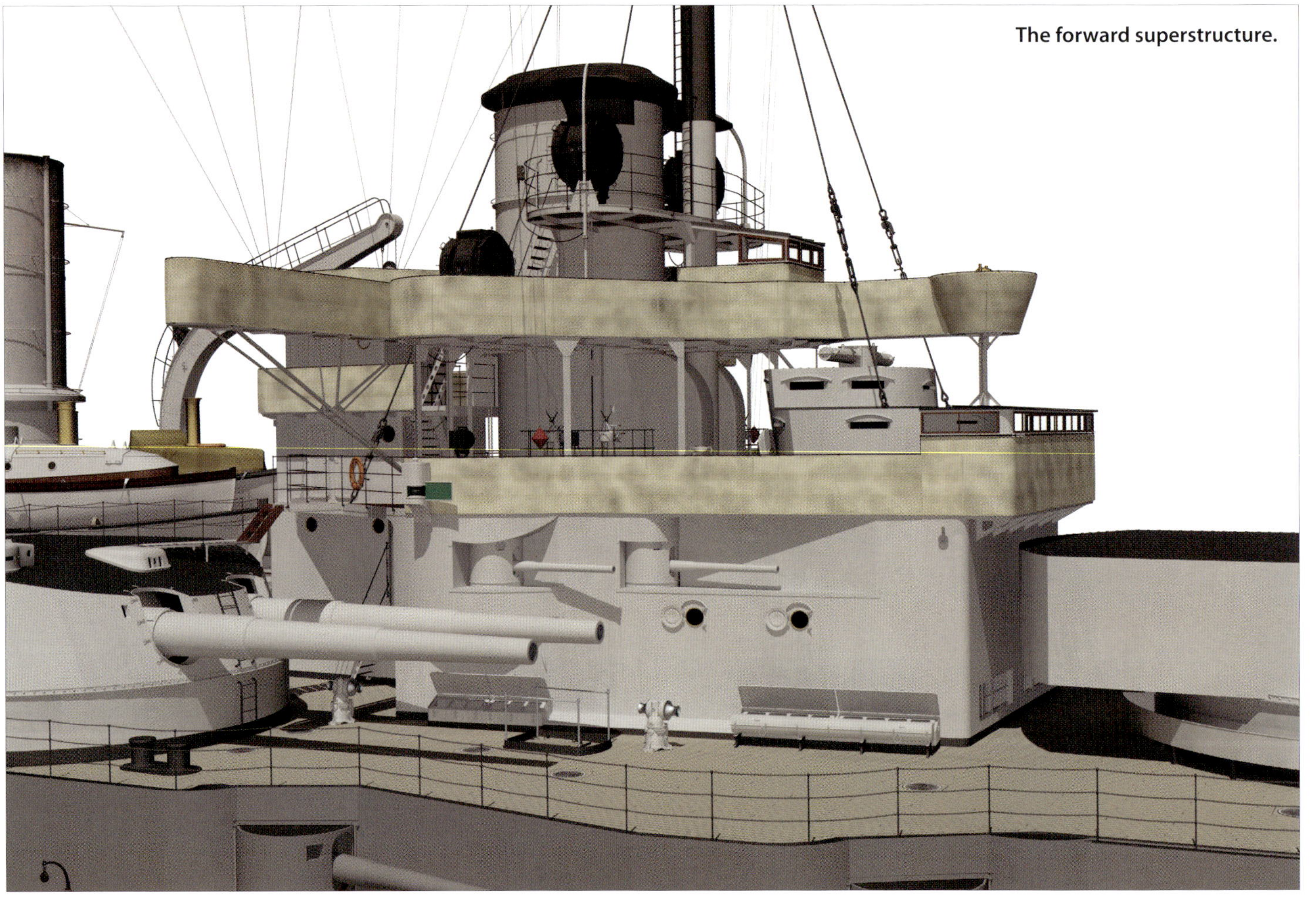
The forward superstructure.

The forward superstructure showing the folding docking bridge.

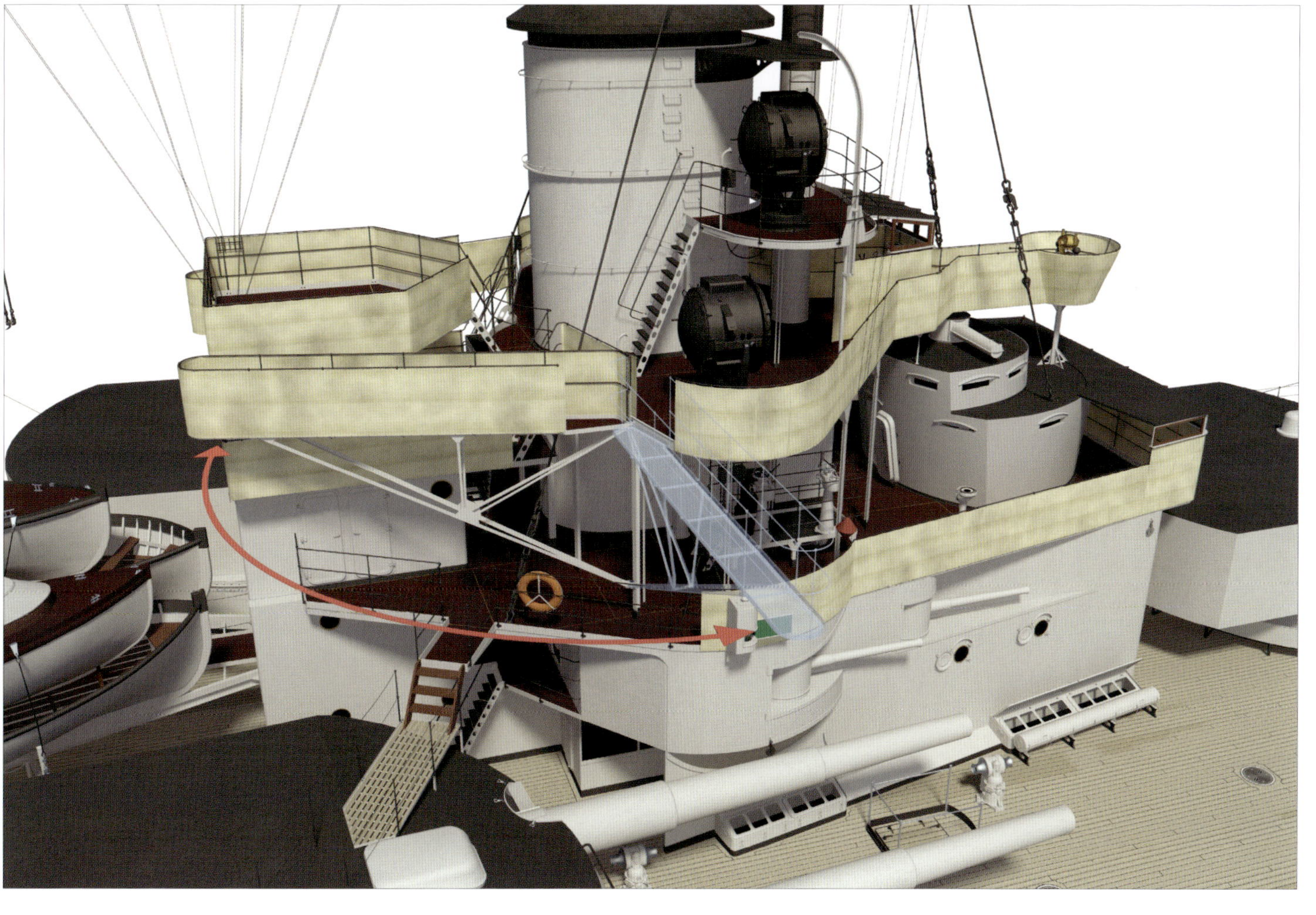

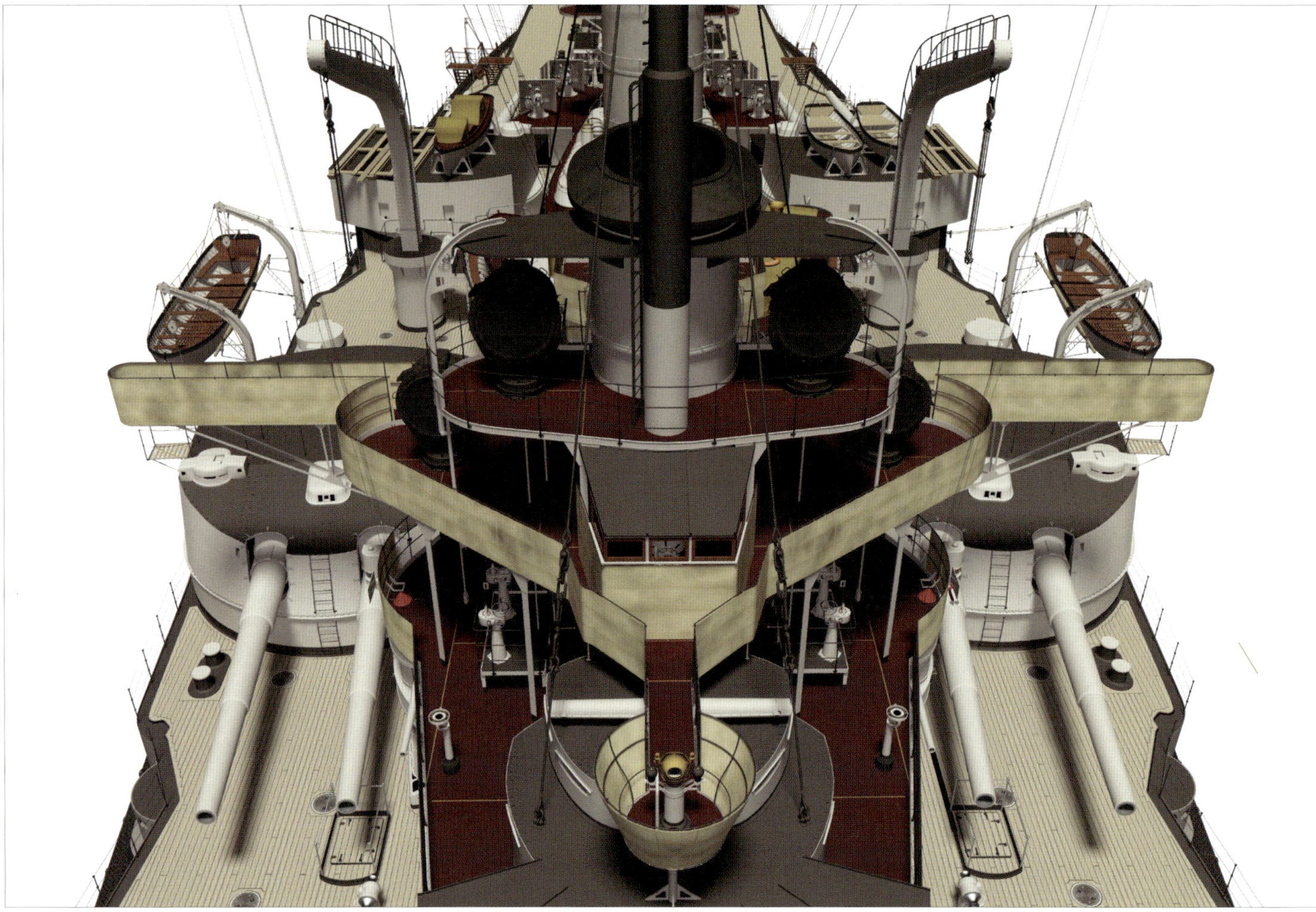

View of the forward superstructure with the canvas screens removed.

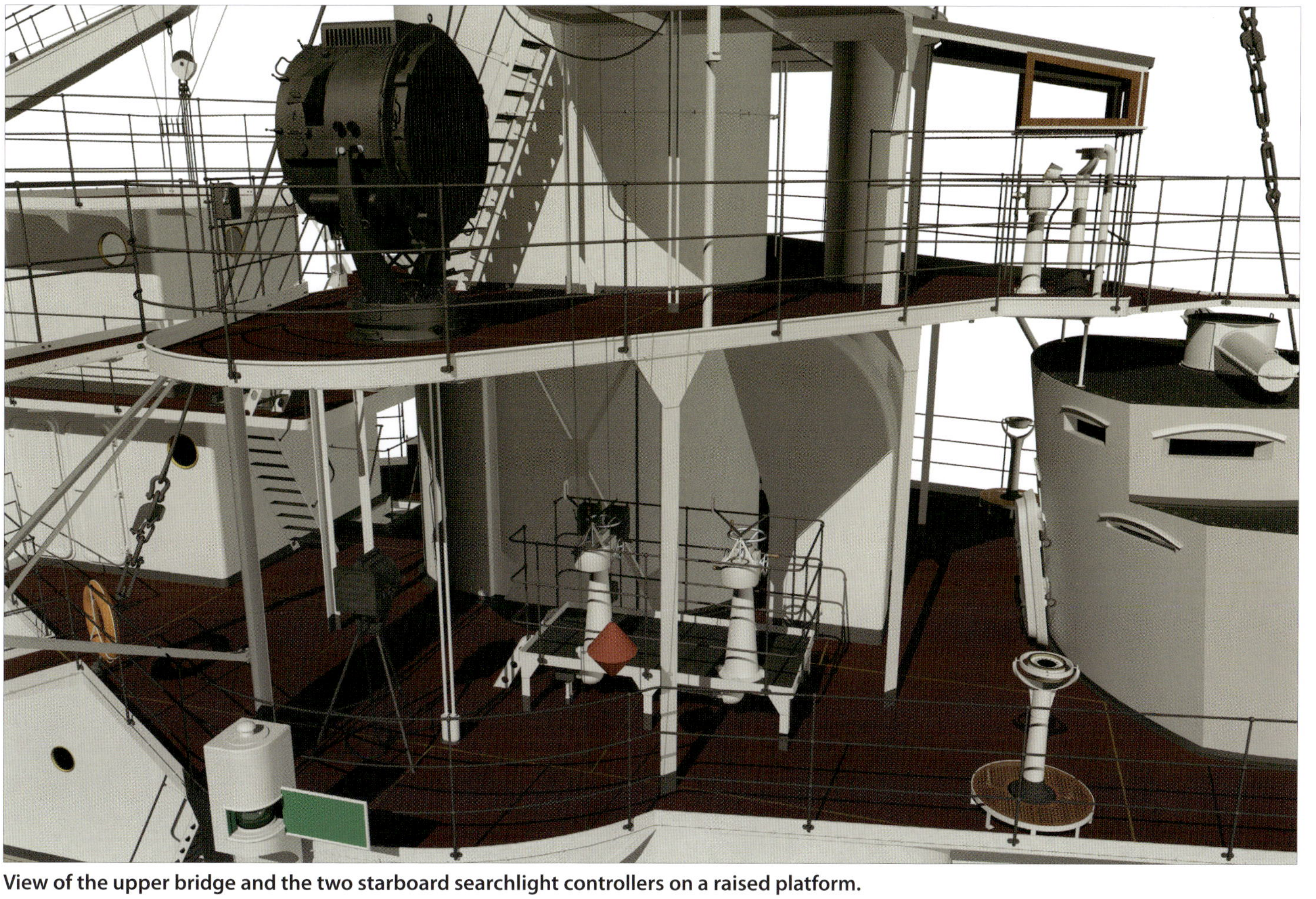

View of the upper bridge and the two starboard searchlight controllers on a raised platform.

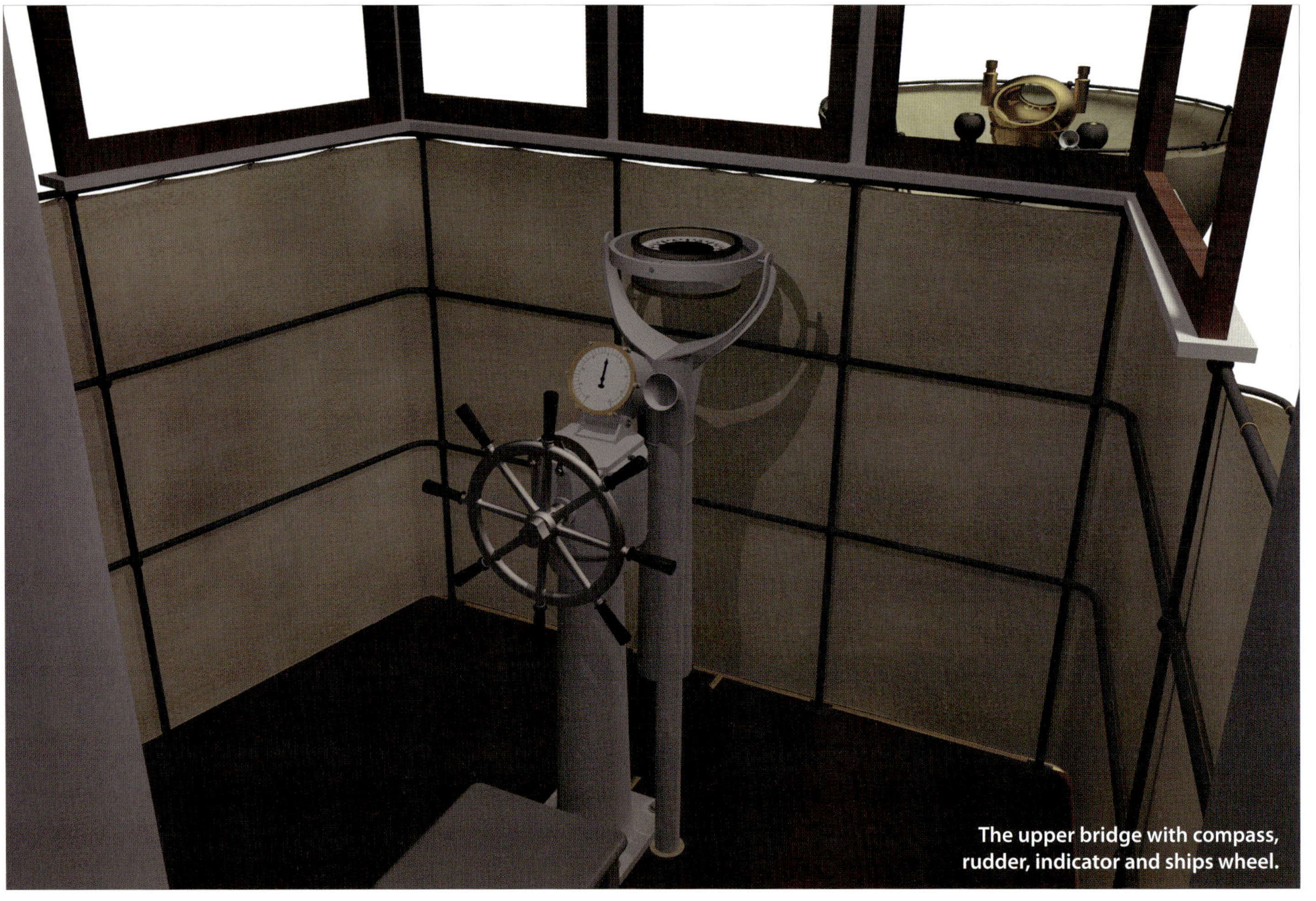

The upper bridge with compass, rudder, indicator and ships wheel.

The forward compass platform.

The door on the left leads to the ship's bakery.

View of the starboard side forward superstructure showing the boiler room air intakes.

Looking across the gangway to the forward superstructure. This rear block was topped by the signals platform below which was the Admiral's day cabin. *Posen* was built as a flagship and so the only one of its class with this upper cabin. Beneath the Admiral's cabin was the Captain's day cabin and the chart house. Below this was a corridor between two store rooms containing the navigation charts.

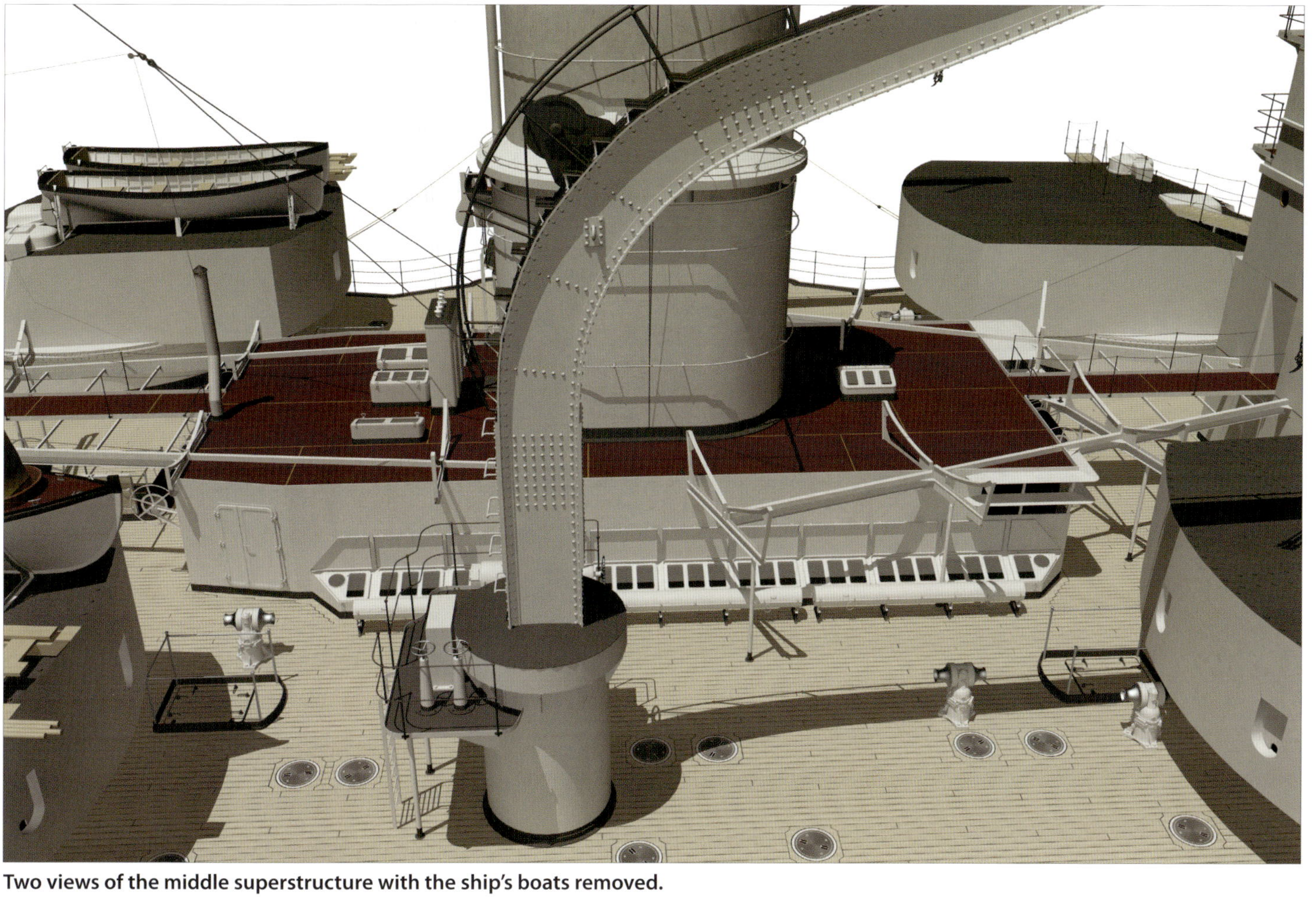

Two views of the middle superstructure with the ship's boats removed.

View of the aft side of the middle superstructure.

View of the forward side of the middle superstructure.

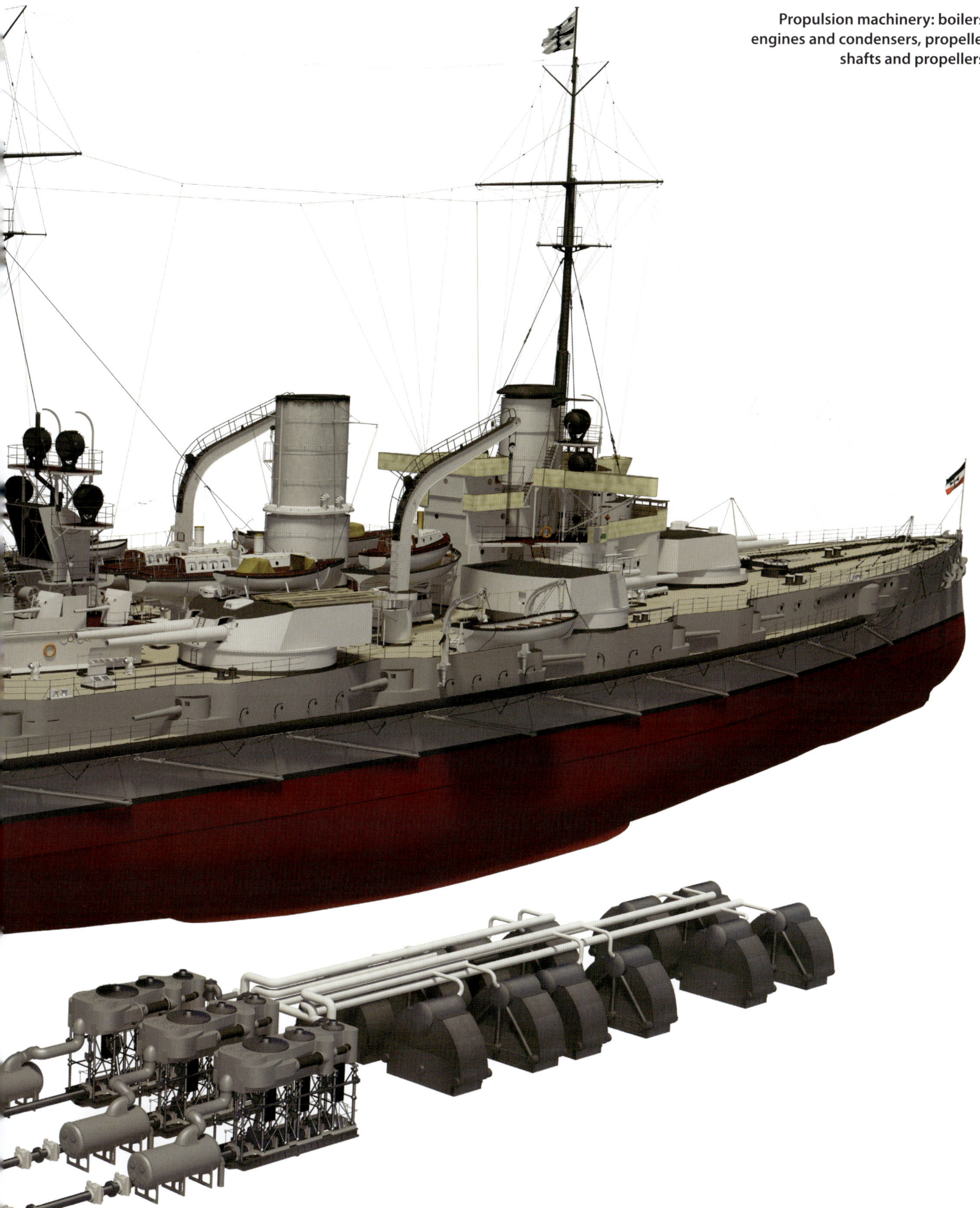

Propulsion machinery: boilers, engines and condensers, propeller shafts and propellers.

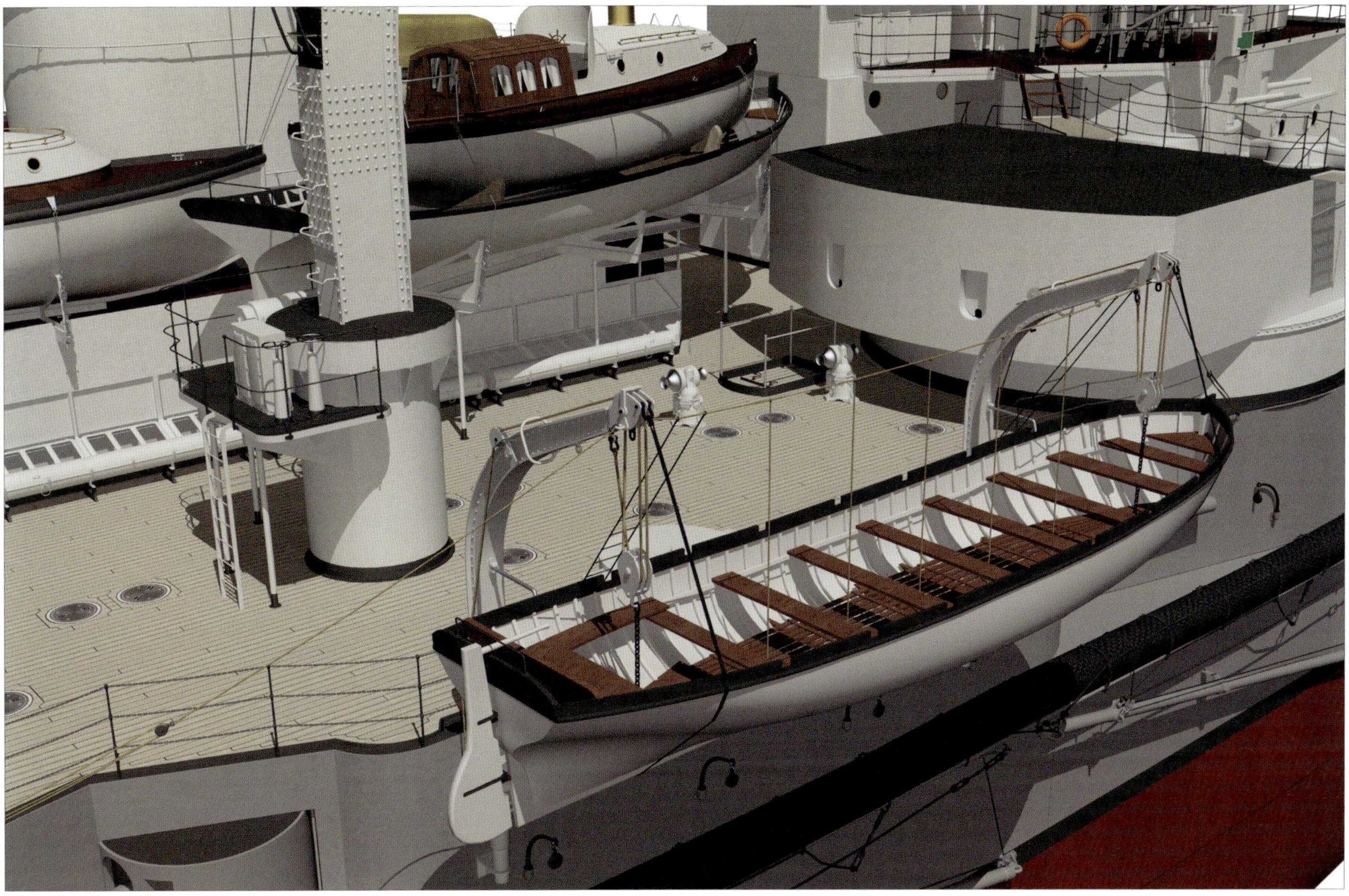

Starboard side, cutter and davits.

Port side, cutter and davits. The round casing of the optical rangefinder for the port 15 cm middle artillery. Coal loading manhole covers an electric coal hoist.

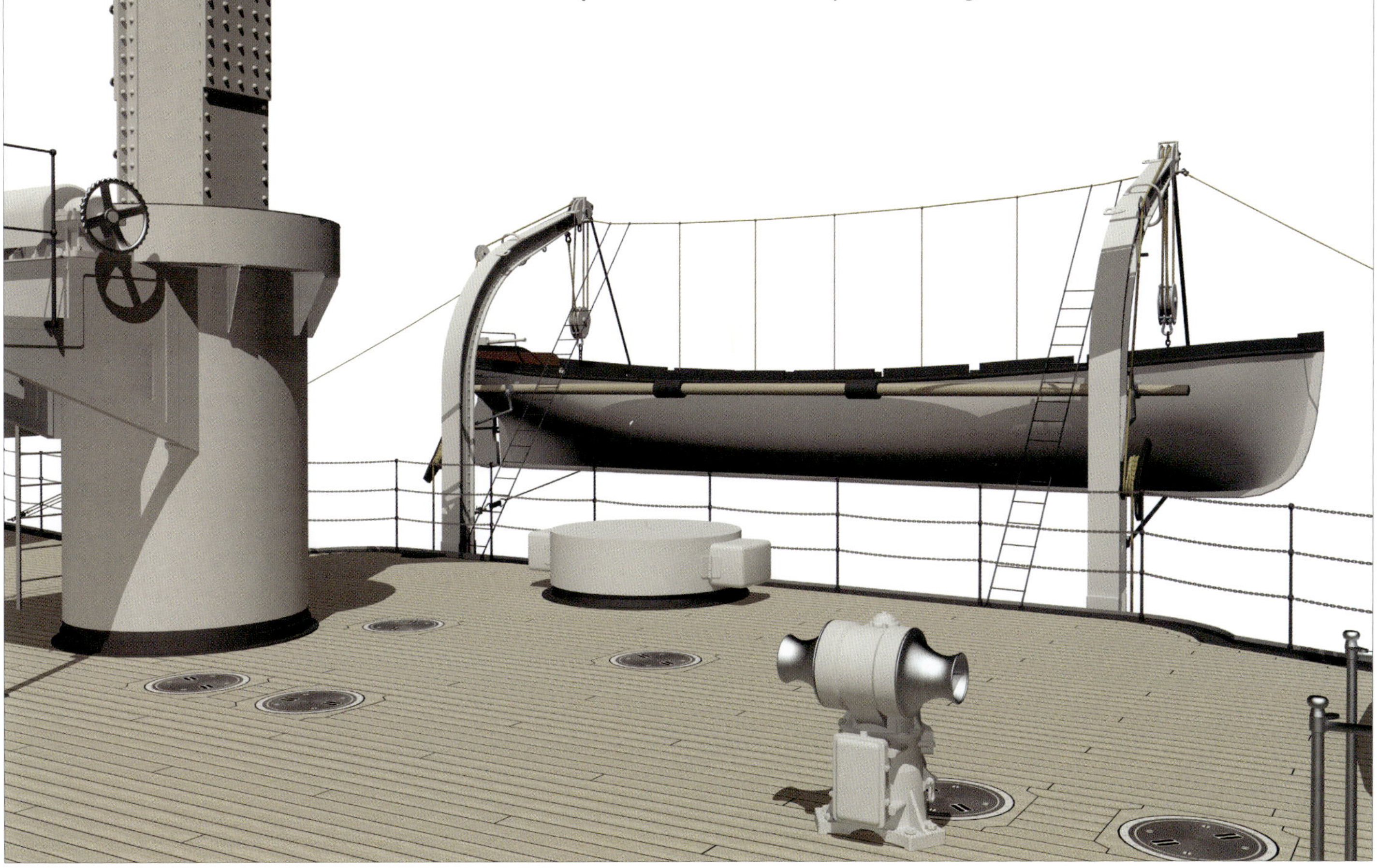

Alongside C turret looking aft.

A view of the rear superstructure looking aft.

Looking forward from a position on the rear superstructure.

The searchlight controllers were used to remotely rotate and elevate the searchlights preventing the crews from being blinded by the strong light.

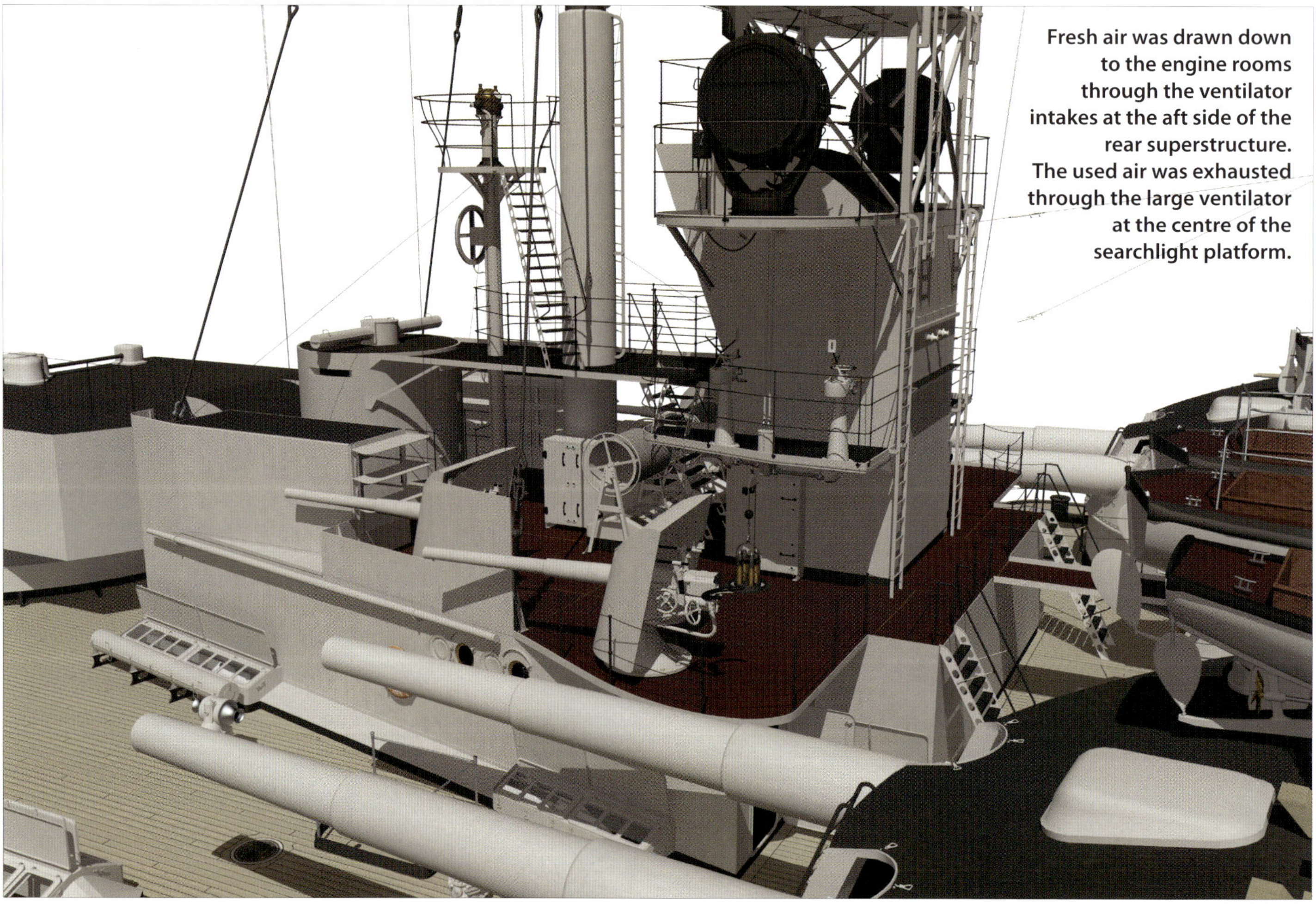

Fresh air was drawn down to the engine rooms through the ventilator intakes at the aft side of the rear superstructure. The used air was exhausted through the large ventilator at the centre of the searchlight platform.

Rear superstructure showing the raised compass platform which was removed before WW1.

Rear superstructure and the rear conning tower.

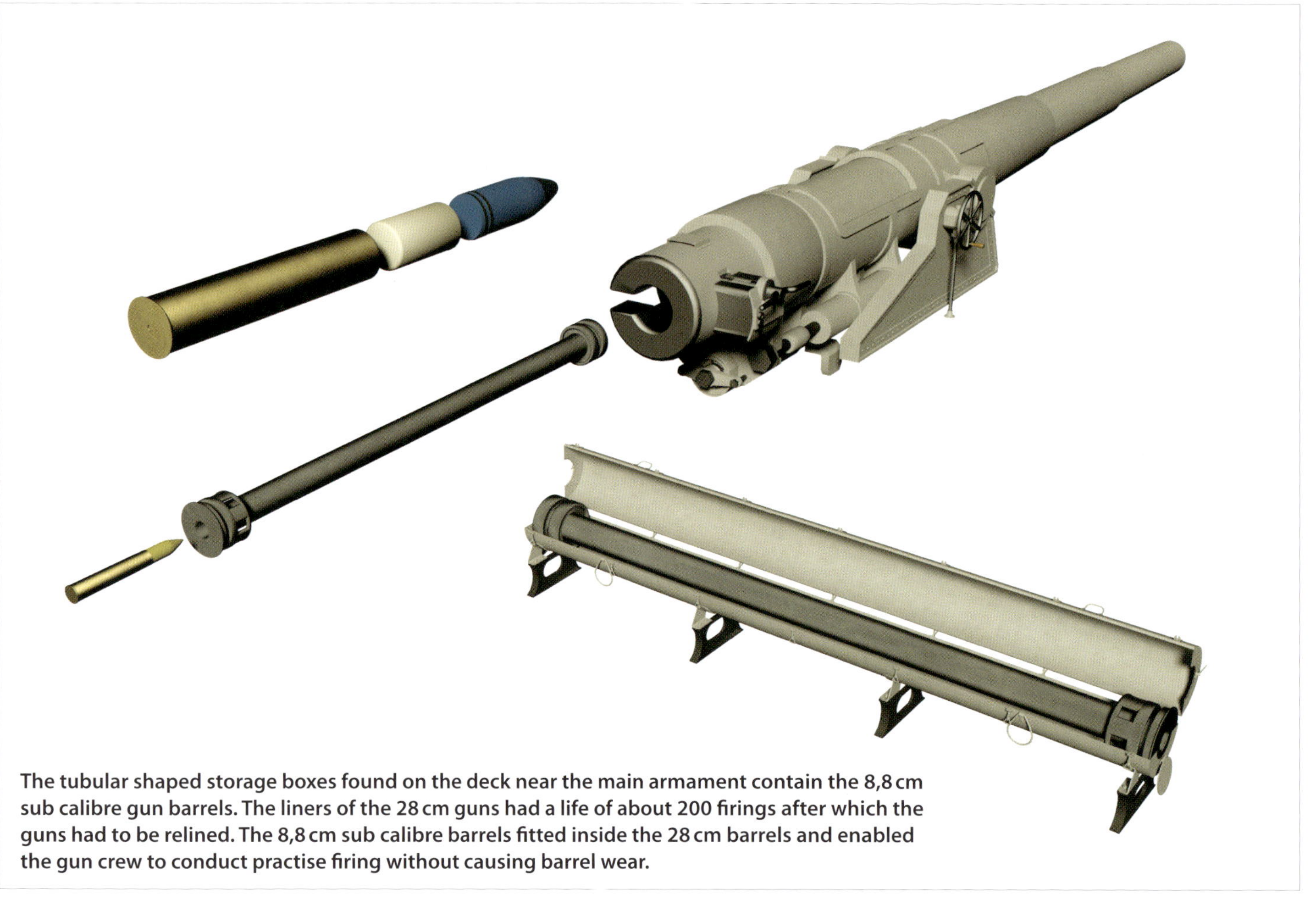

The tubular shaped storage boxes found on the deck near the main armament contain the 8,8 cm sub calibre gun barrels. The liners of the 28 cm guns had a life of about 200 firings after which the guns had to be relined. The 8,8 cm sub calibre barrels fitted inside the 28 cm barrels and enabled the gun crew to conduct practise firing without causing barrel wear.

View from the rear superstructure platform. 8,8 ammunition lift, cable drum and conning tower.

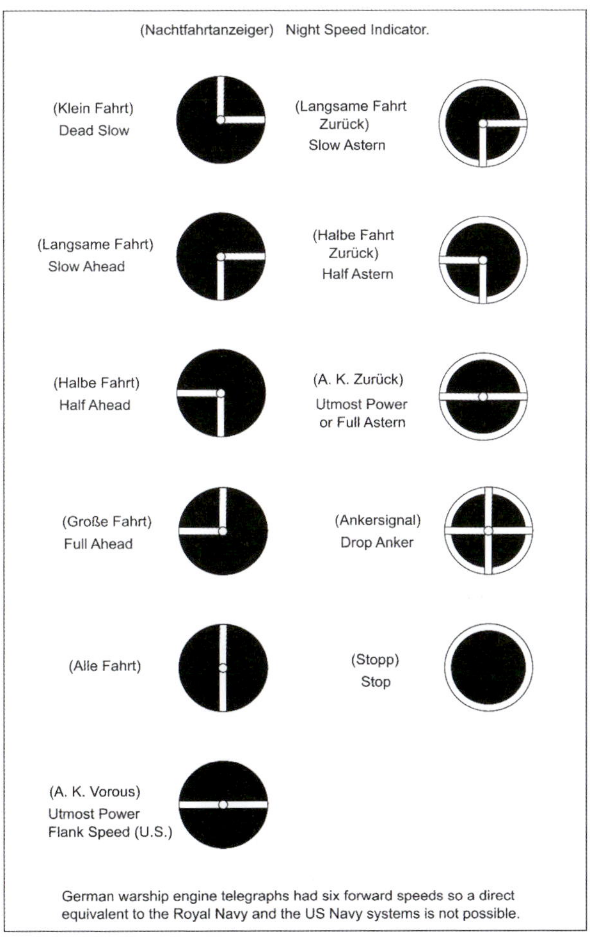

The Night Speed Indicator (Nachtfahrtanzeiger) was used to order speed changes to the fleet sailing in line ahead formation during the hours of darkness. The device used rows of small light bulbs which could be illuminated giving eleven different symbols. Each symbol corresponding to a position on the engine telegraph ranging from full speed ahead to full astern. These signal devices were usually mounted on the rear superstructure or the rear mast so to be clearly visible to the following ship. When a change of speed was ordered each ship repeated the signal allowing the fleet to maintain the same speed. At the time German warship engine telegraphs had six forward speeds, so direct equivalents to the Royal Navy and US Navy system are not possible.

C Turret (right) and D turret (left) and the rear superstructure seen from the aft deck.

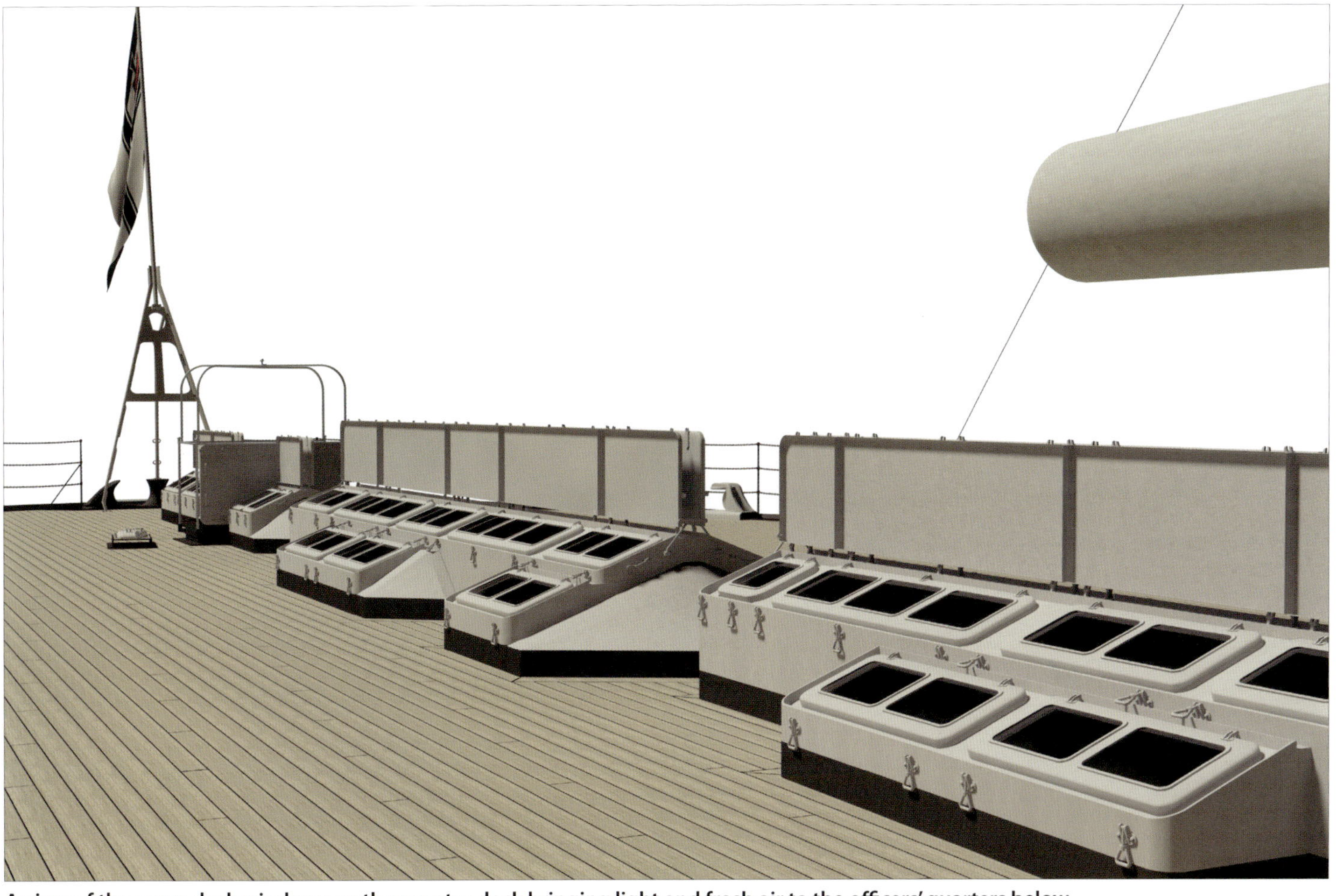

A view of the many deck windows on the quarter deck bringing light and fresh air to the officers' quarters below.

Removable stairway on the face of D turret.
Capstan with steam valve and one of the four bollards on the quarter deck.

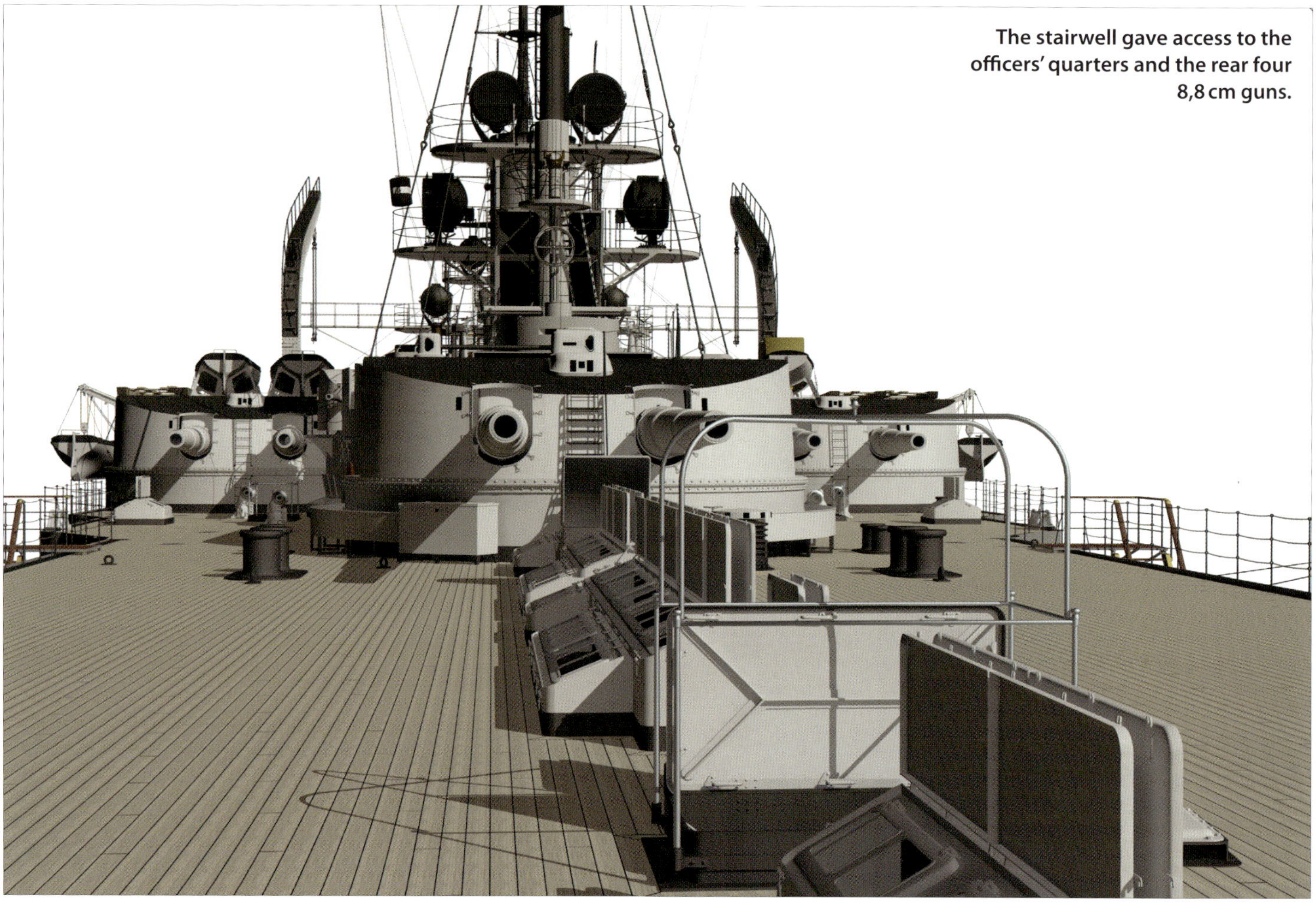

The stairwell gave access to the officers' quarters and the rear four 8,8 cm guns.

Around A and D turrets was a trough like container used to catch the ejected brass 28 cm casings. This was later removed.

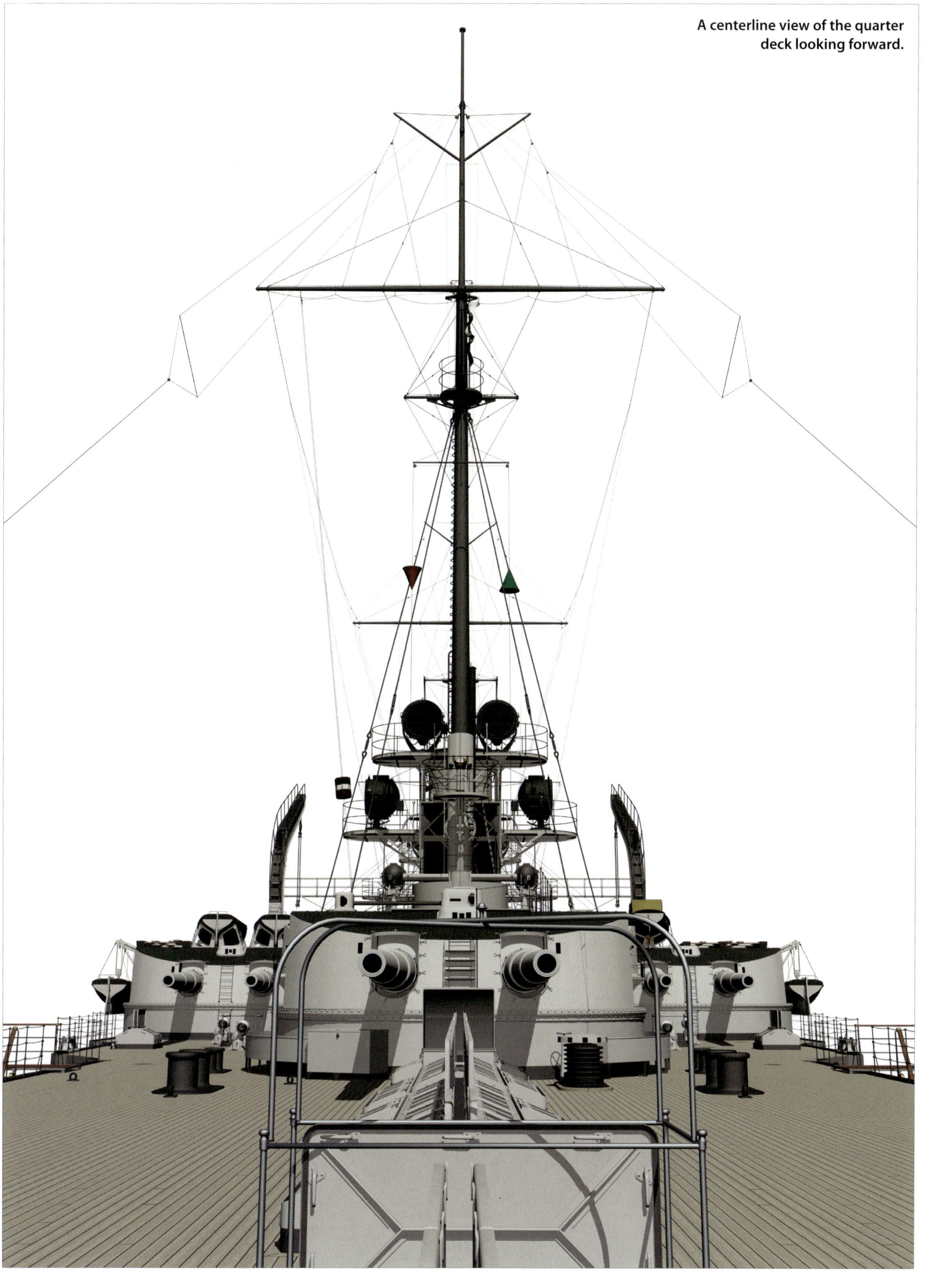

A centerline view of the quarter deck looking forward.

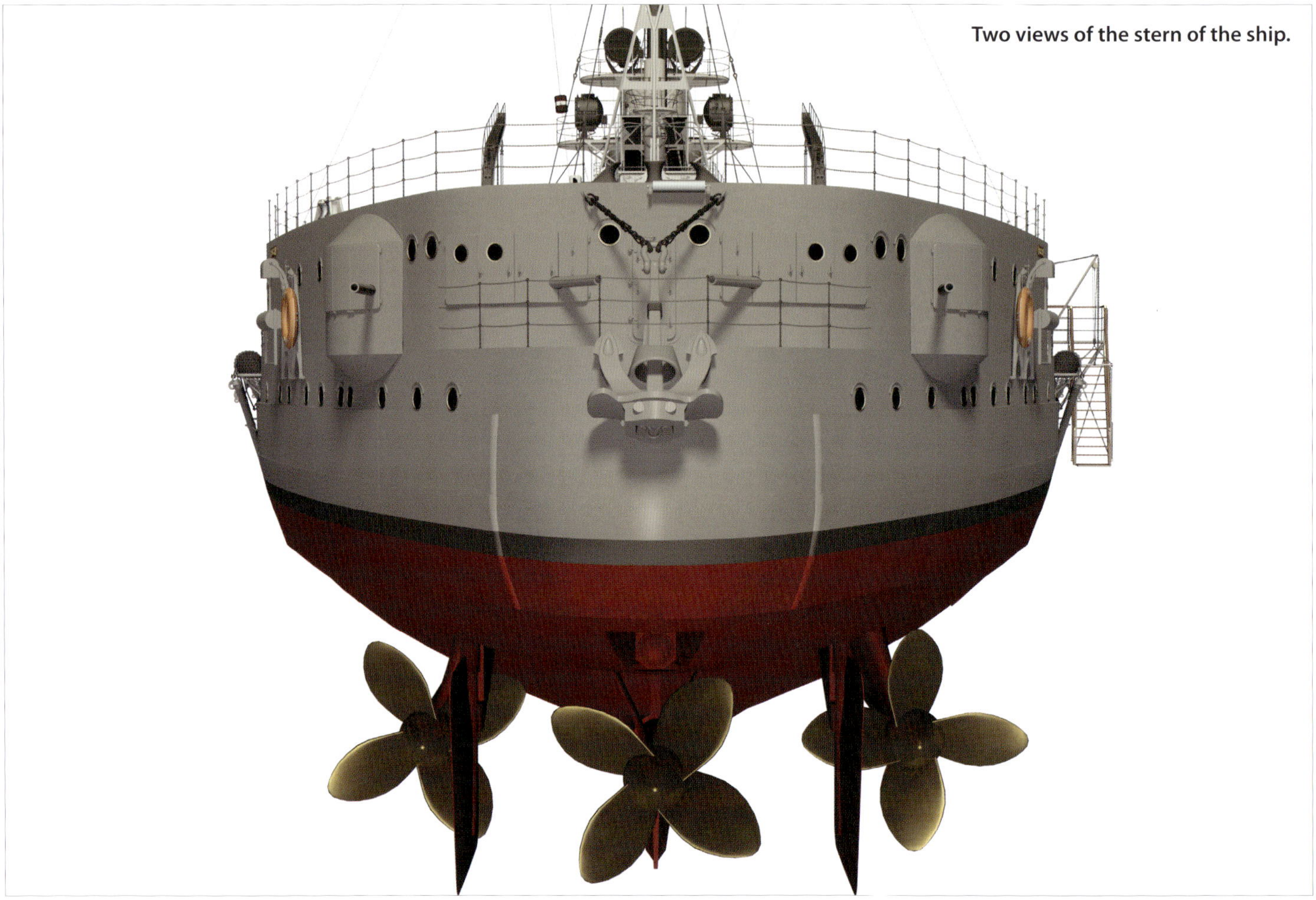

Two views of the stern of the ship.

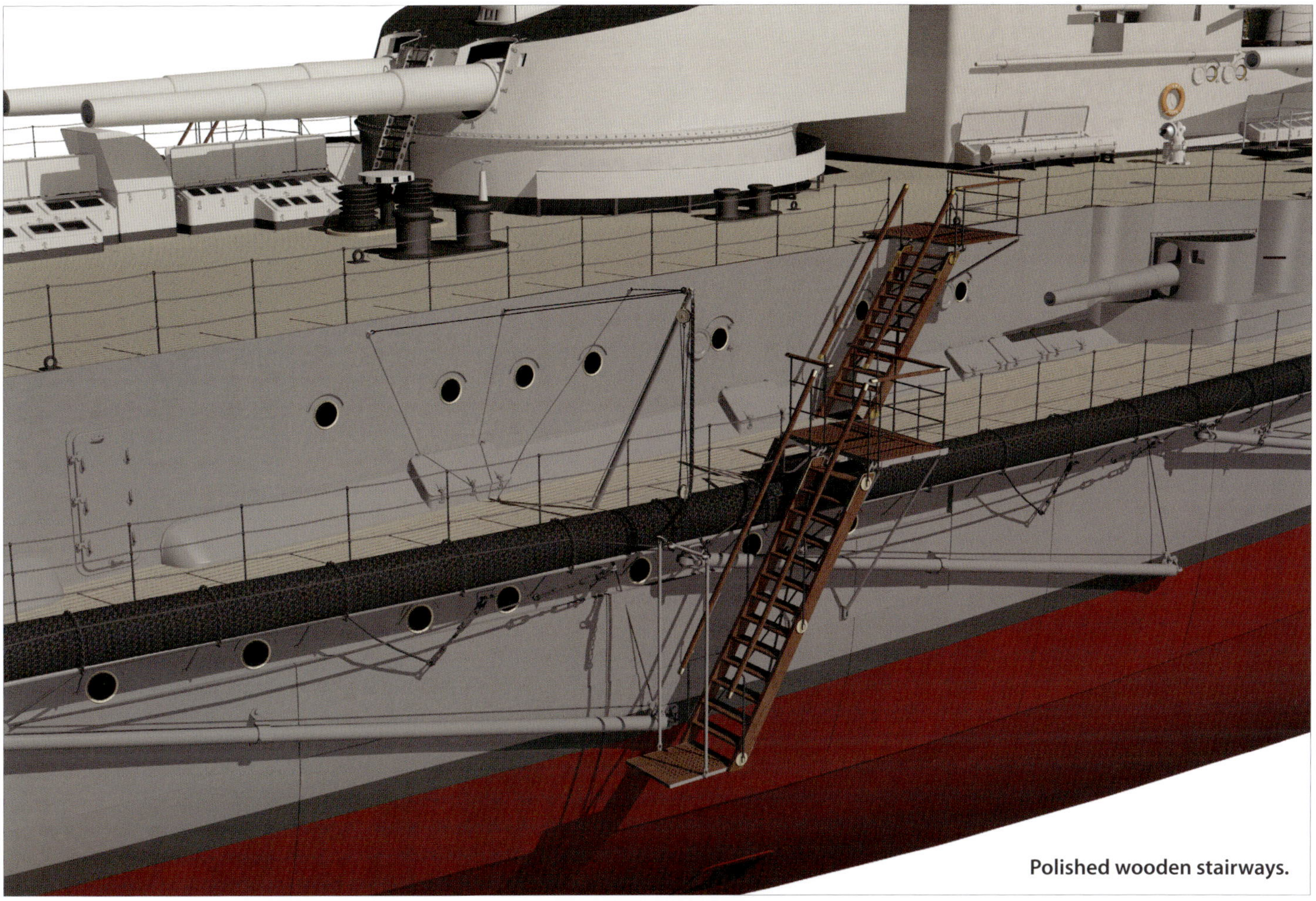

Polished wooden stairways.

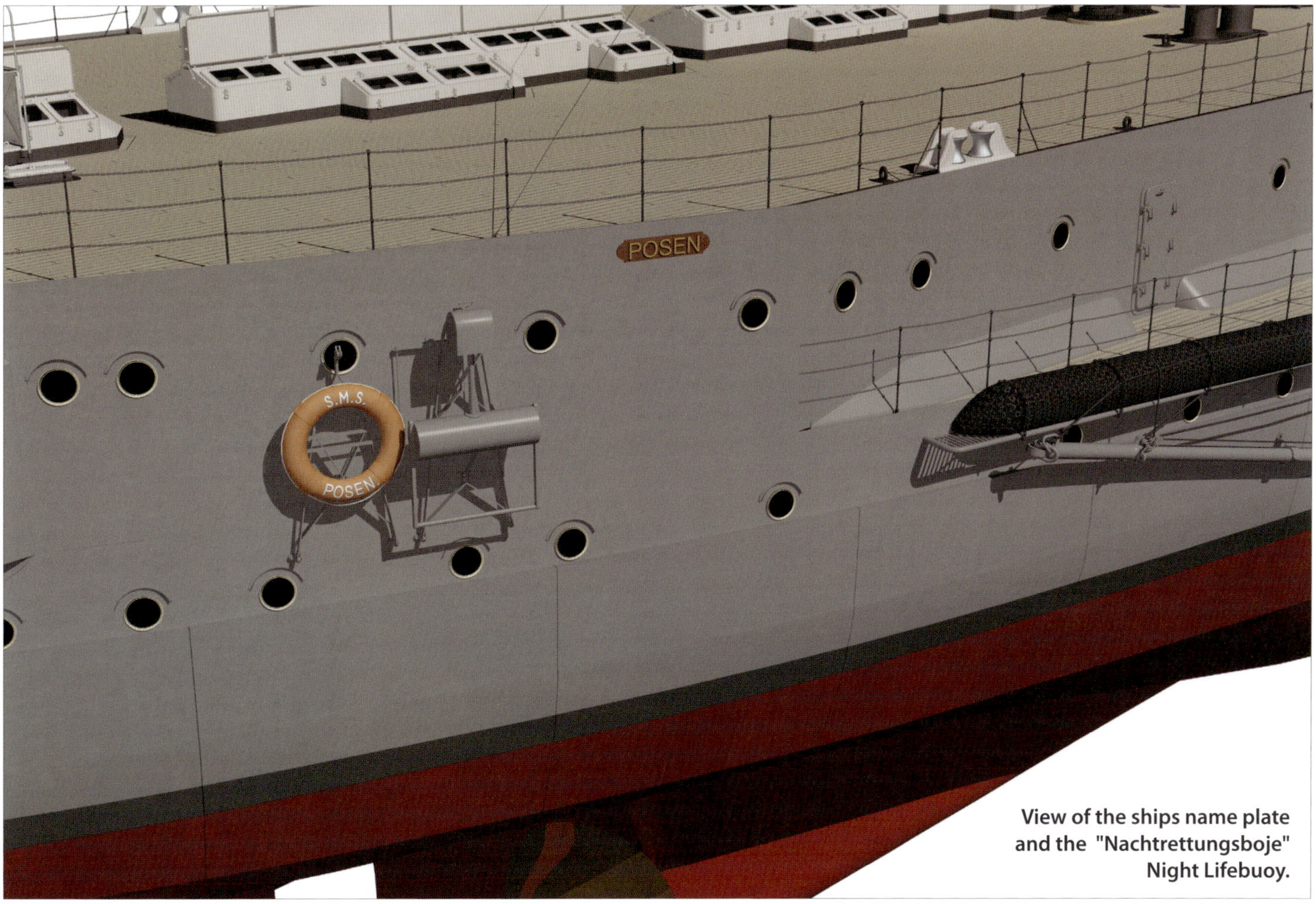

View of the ships name plate and the "Nachtrettungsboje" Night Lifebuoy.

POSEN

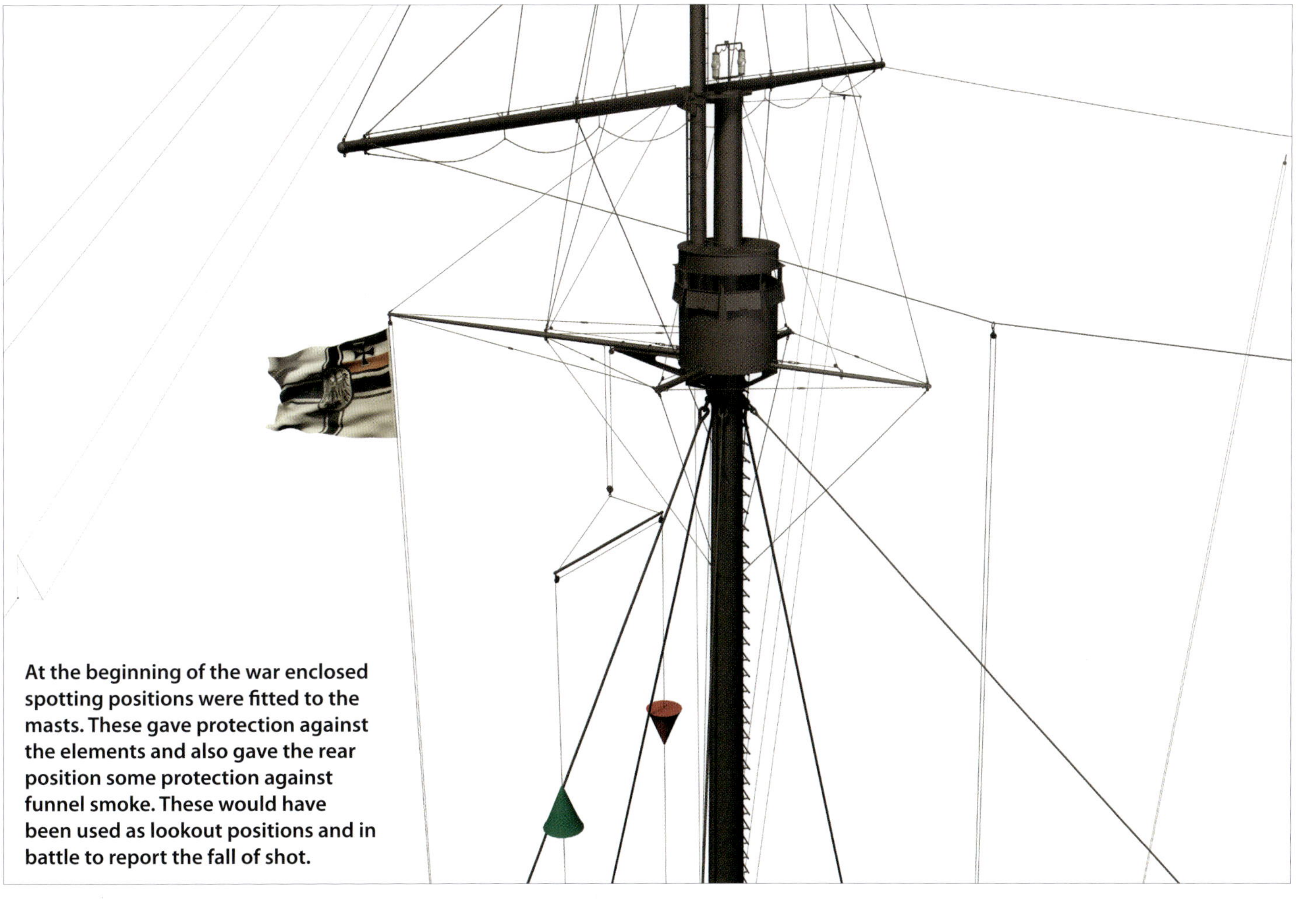

At the beginning of the war enclosed spotting positions were fitted to the masts. These gave protection against the elements and also gave the rear position some protection against funnel smoke. These would have been used as lookout positions and in battle to report the fall of shot.

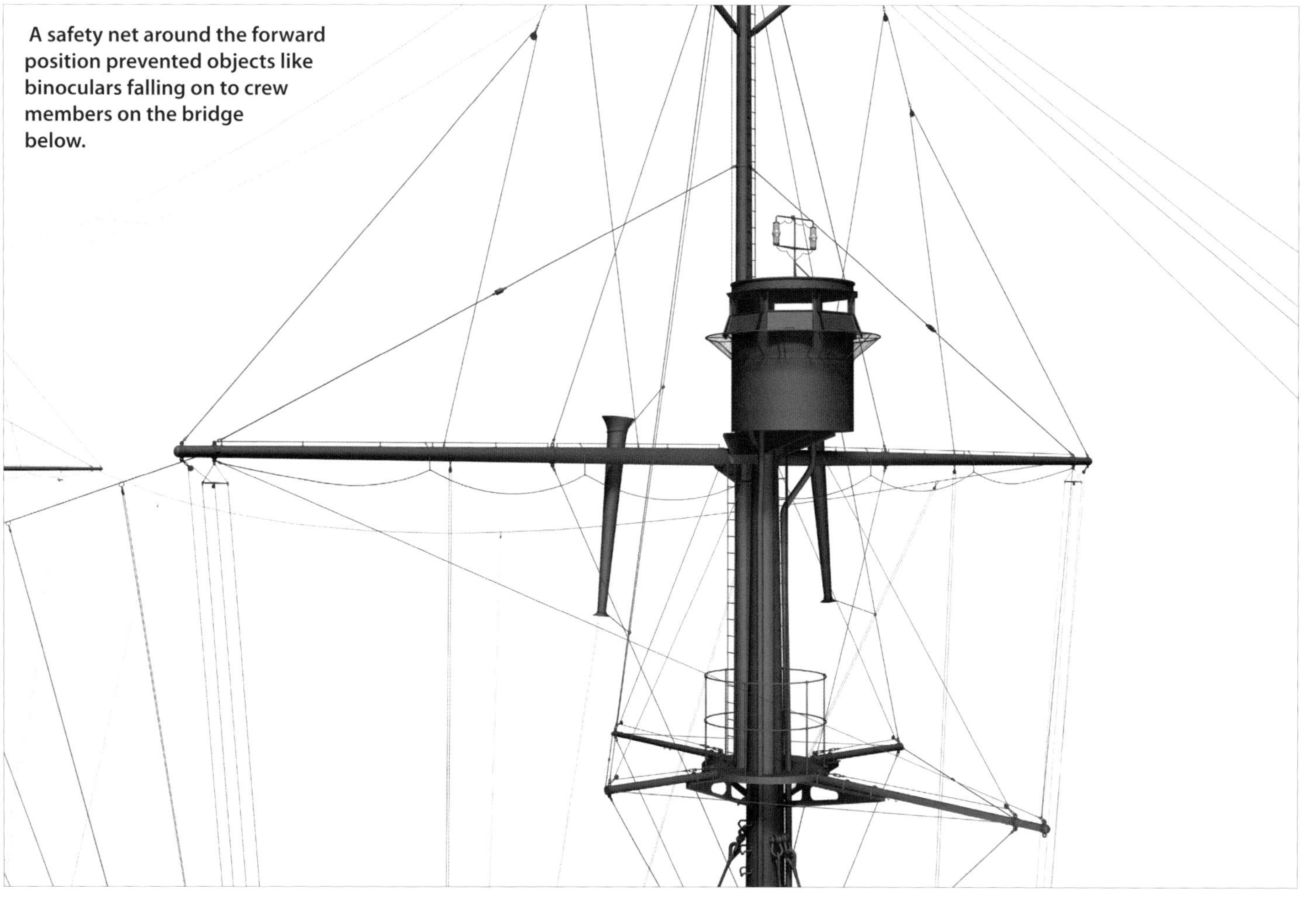

A safety net around the forward position prevented objects like binoculars falling on to crew members on the bridge below.

Four Direction Indicating Periscope's were fitted to the artillery section of the conning tower. The 3 meter periscope was raised to provide enough clearance but this necessitated the removal of the walkway between the upper bridge and the compass platform.

During the war the 8,8 cm guns were removed from the bridge. Also the lower searchlight platforms were extended to be able to fit AA machine guns.

Two internal views showing the direction indicating periscopes.

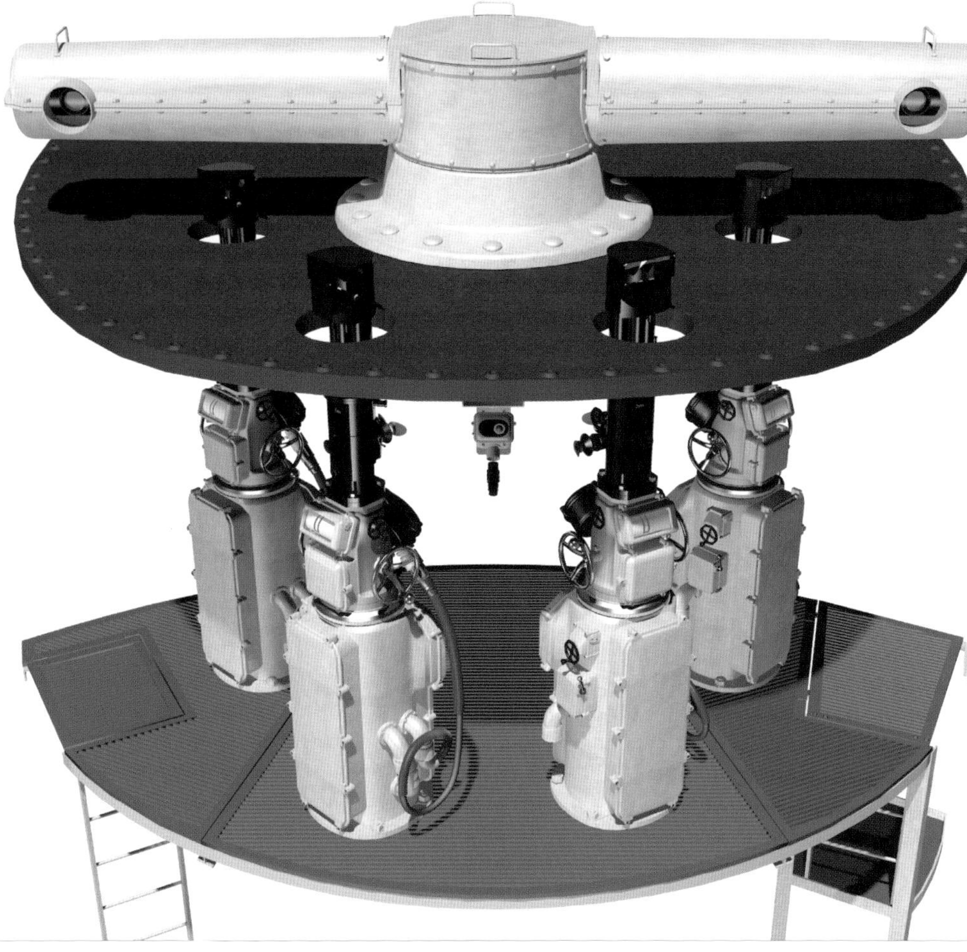

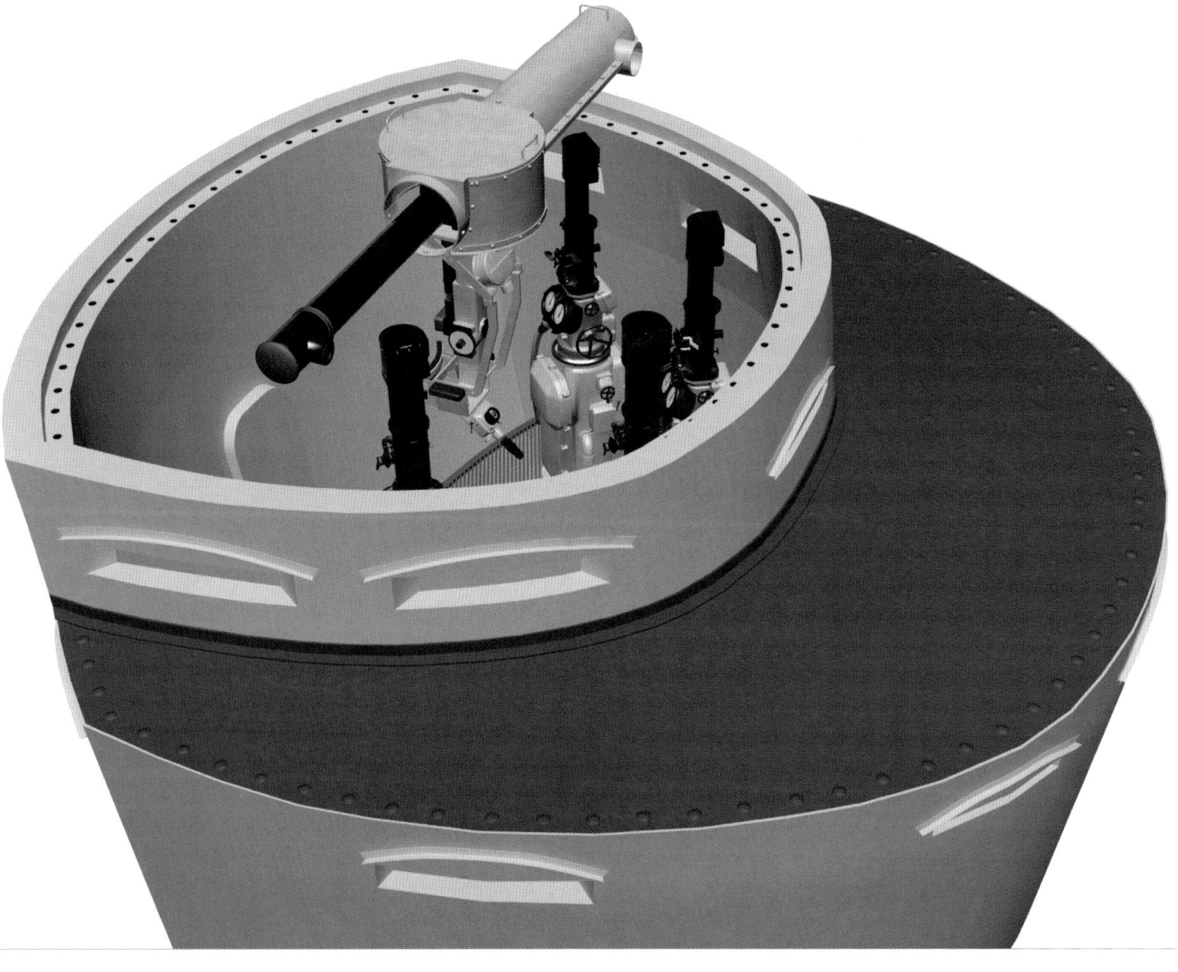

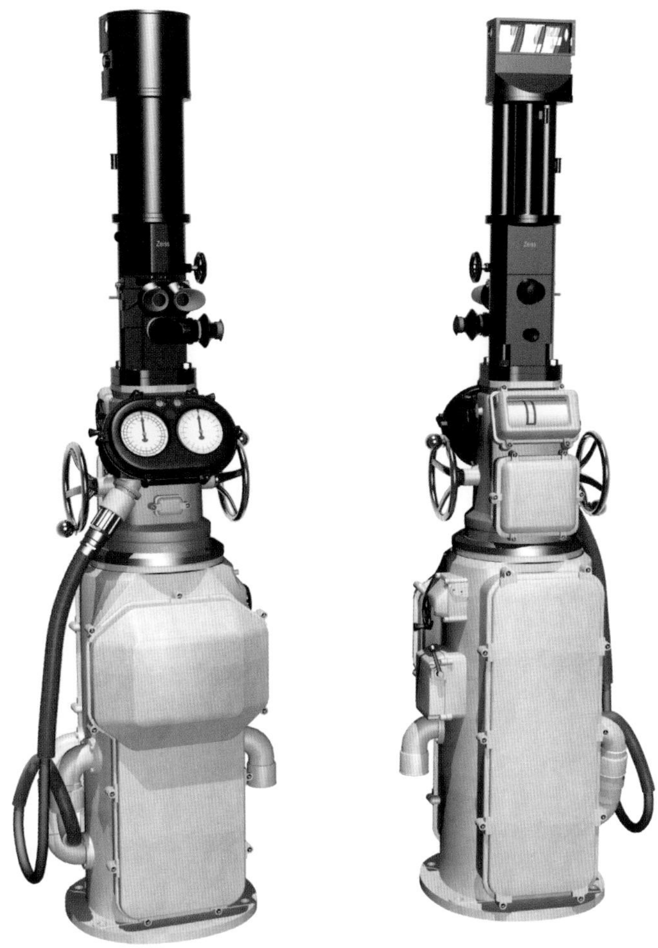

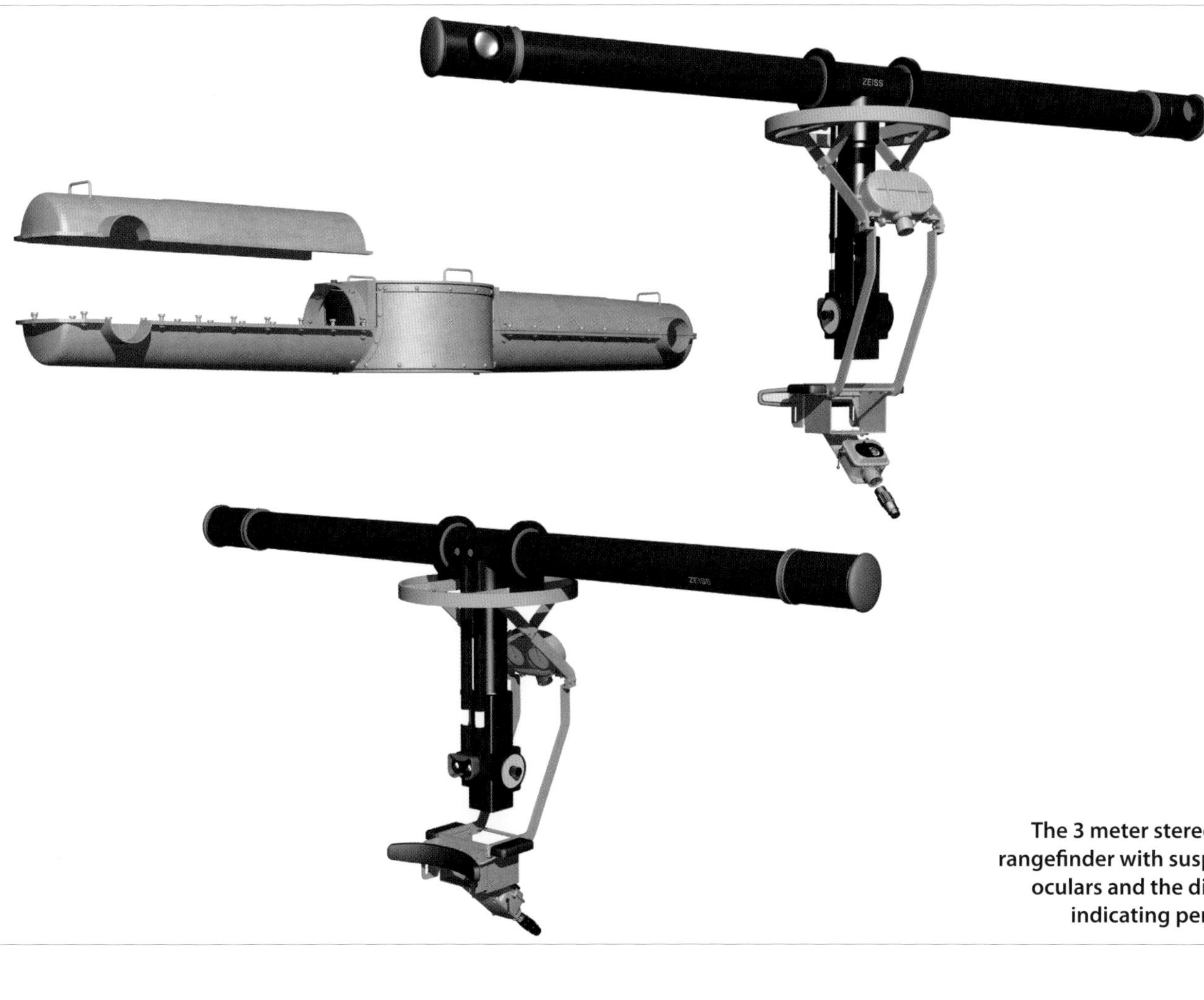

The 3 meter stereoscopic rangefinder with suspended oculars and the direction indicating periscope.

Two Views of the rear superstructure.

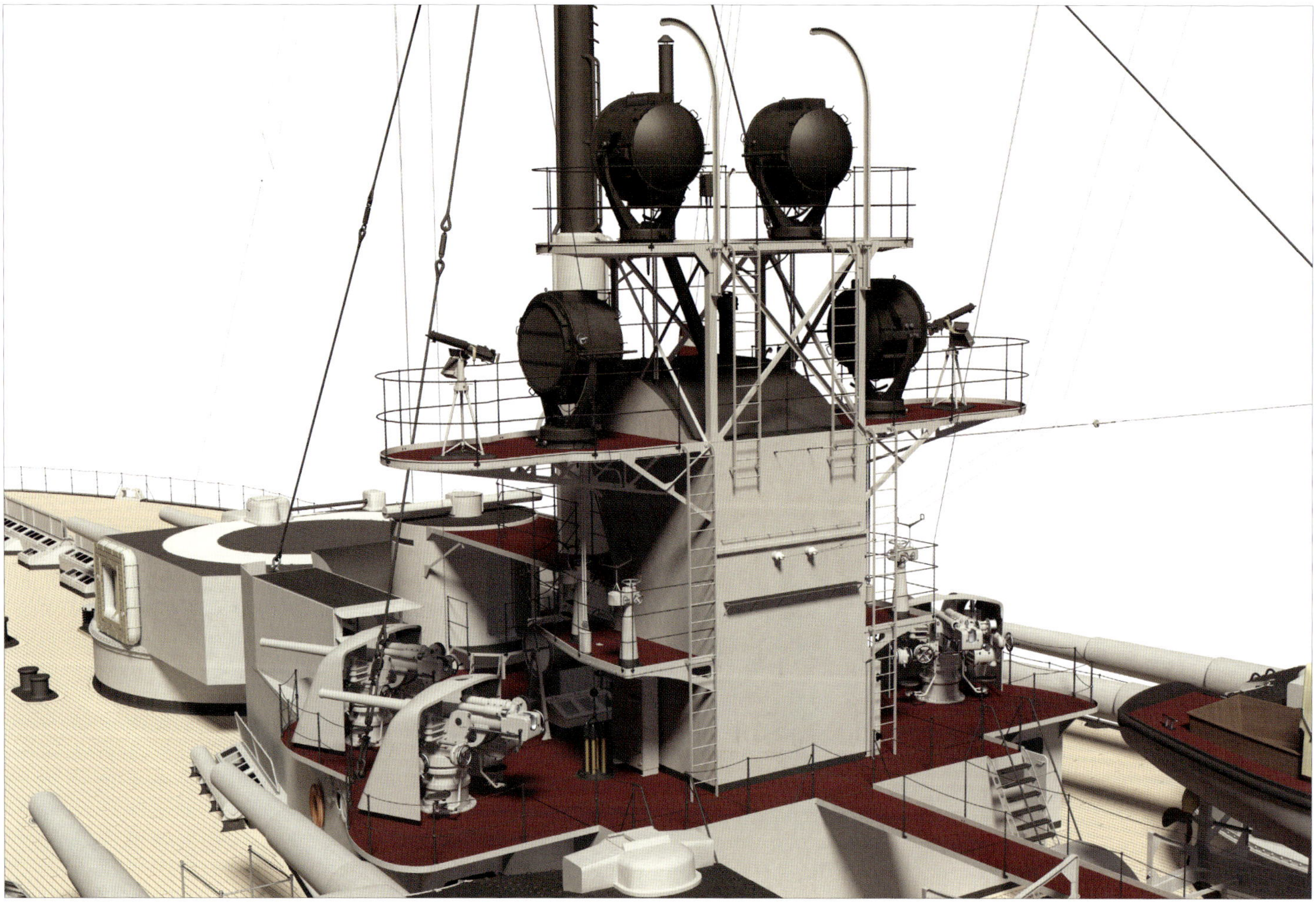

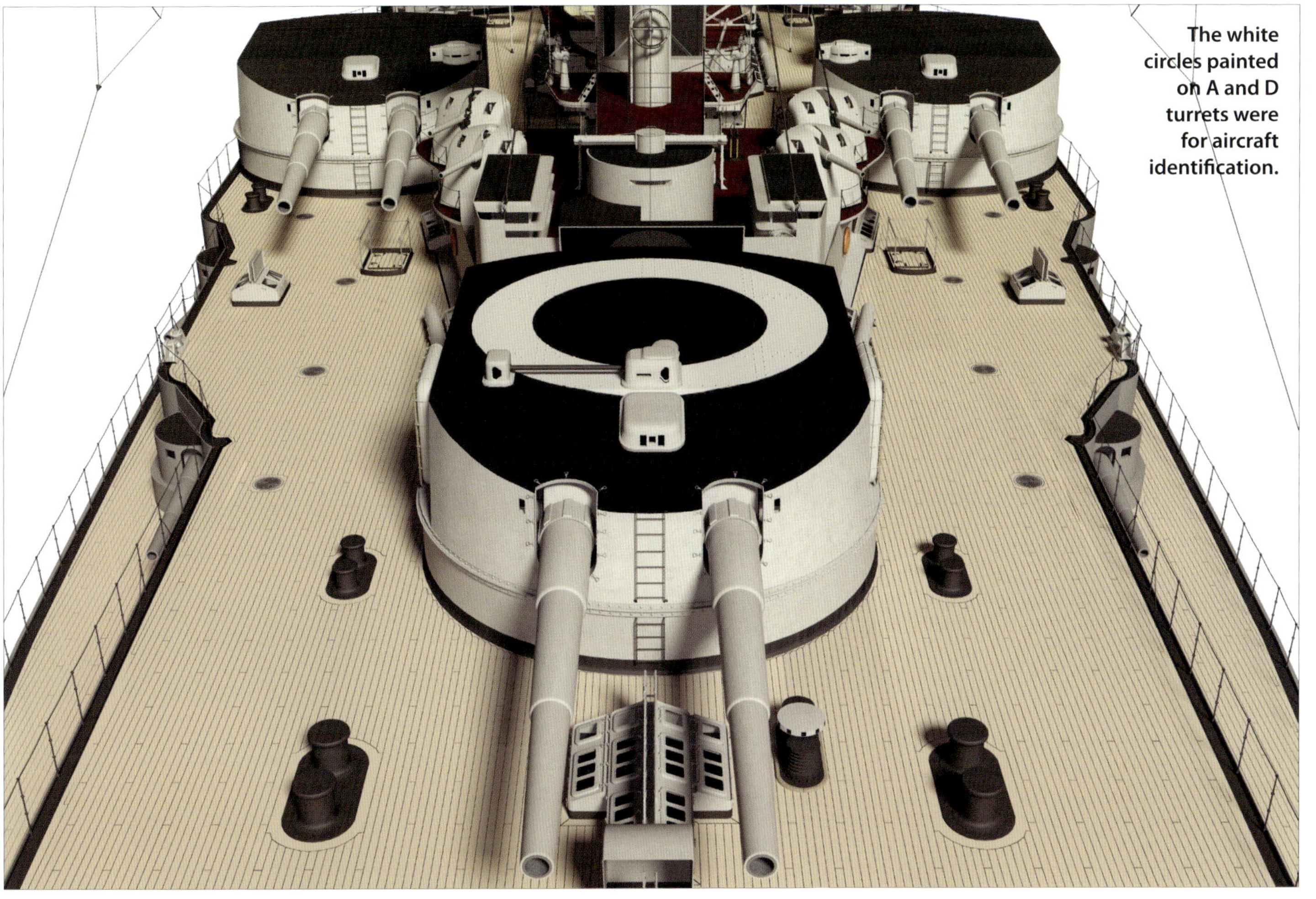

The white circles painted on A and D turrets were for aircraft identification.

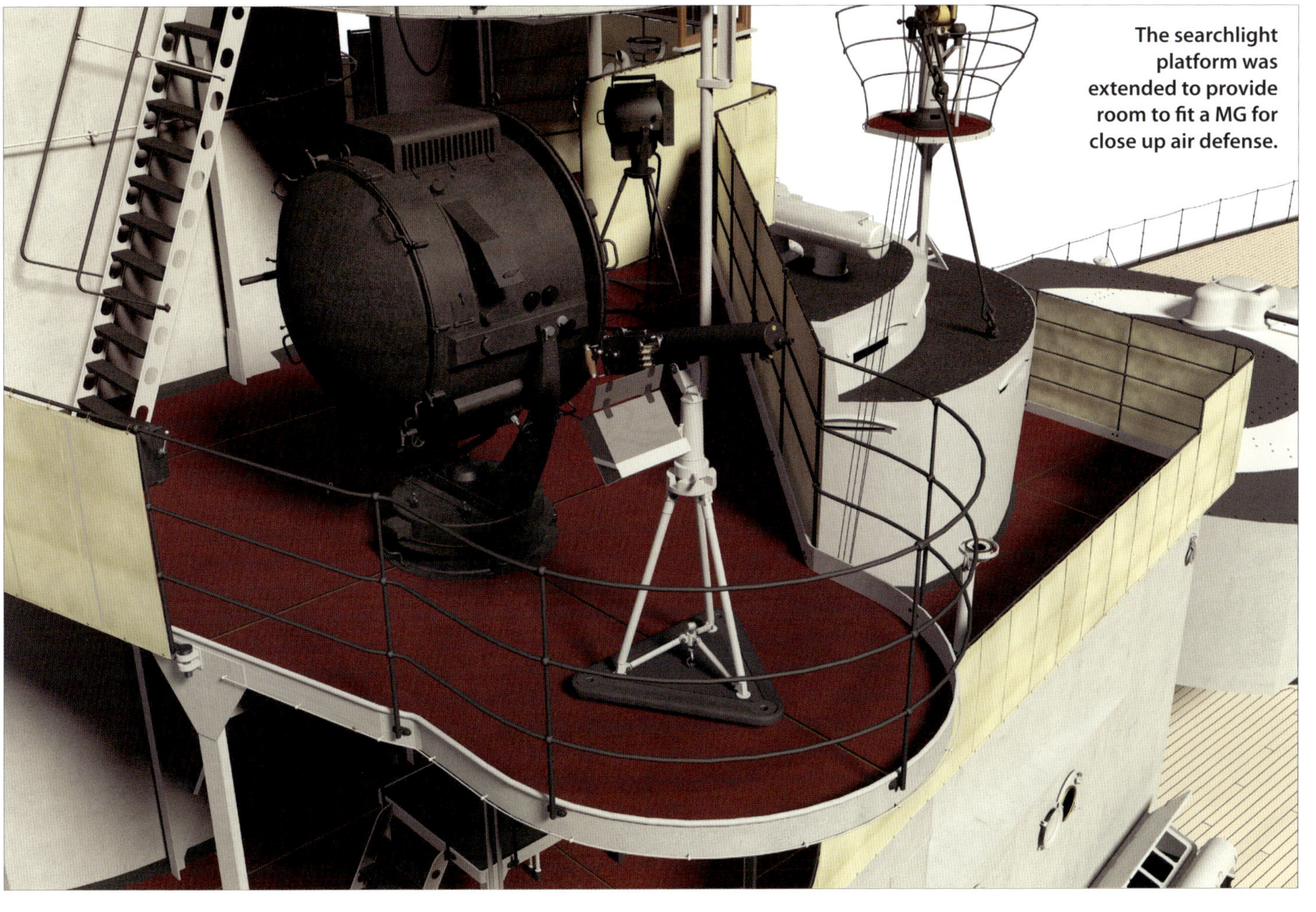

The searchlight platform was extended to provide room to fit a MG for close up air defense.

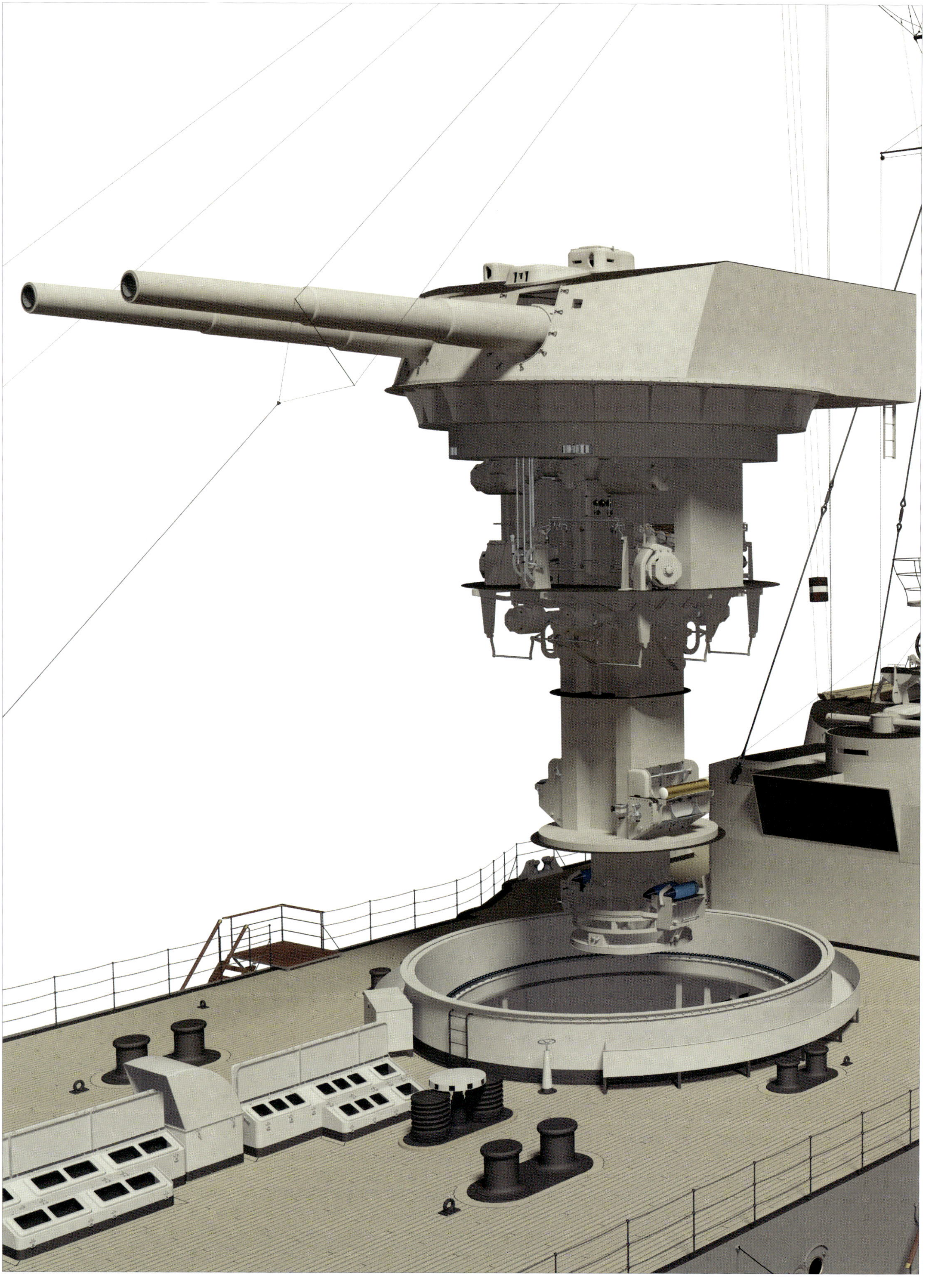

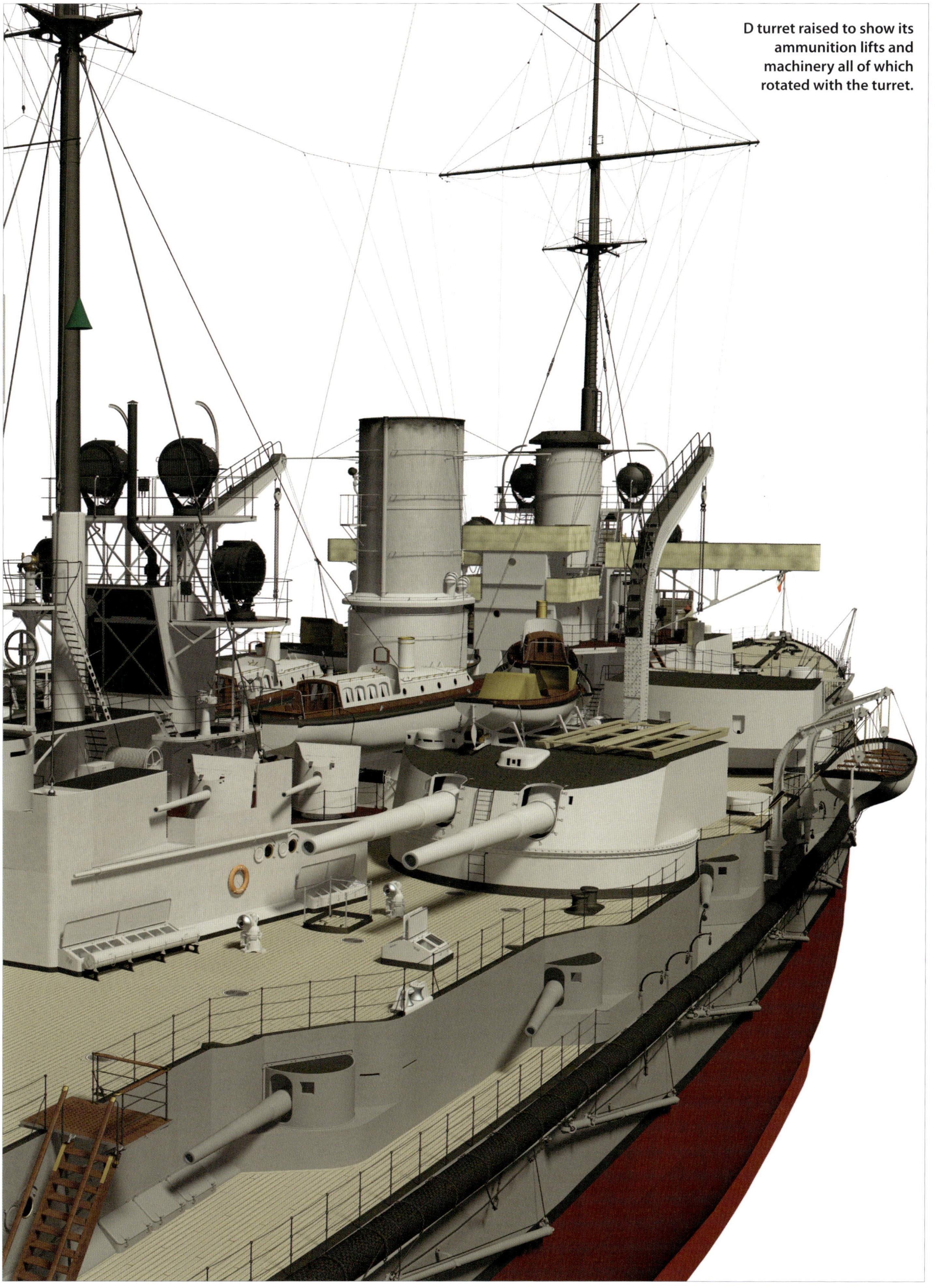

D turret raised to show its ammunition lifts and machinery all of which rotated with the turret.

The centerline (A and D) 28 cm turrets with their platforms lifts and machinery.

Two views of the 28 cm SK L/45 turret.

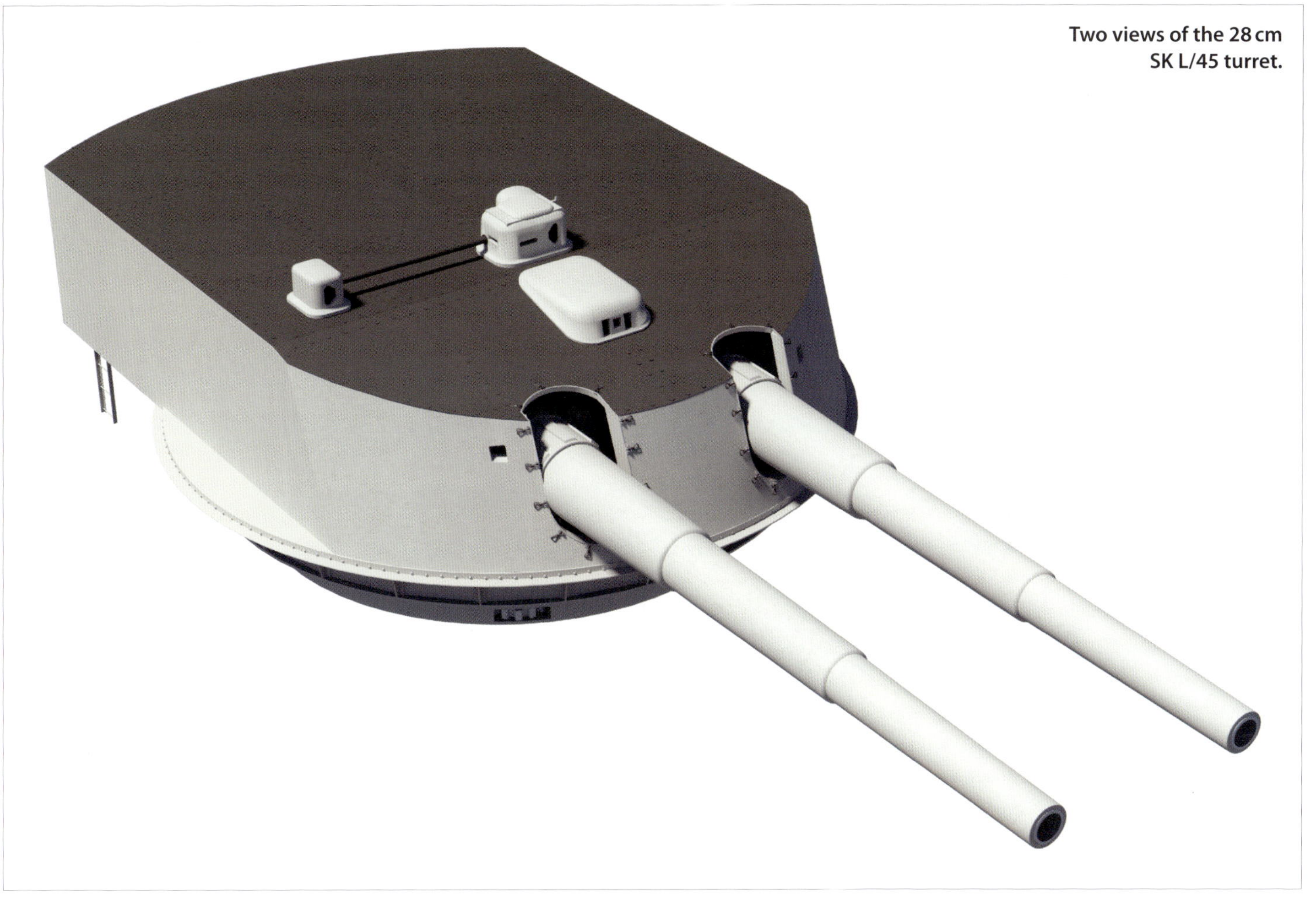

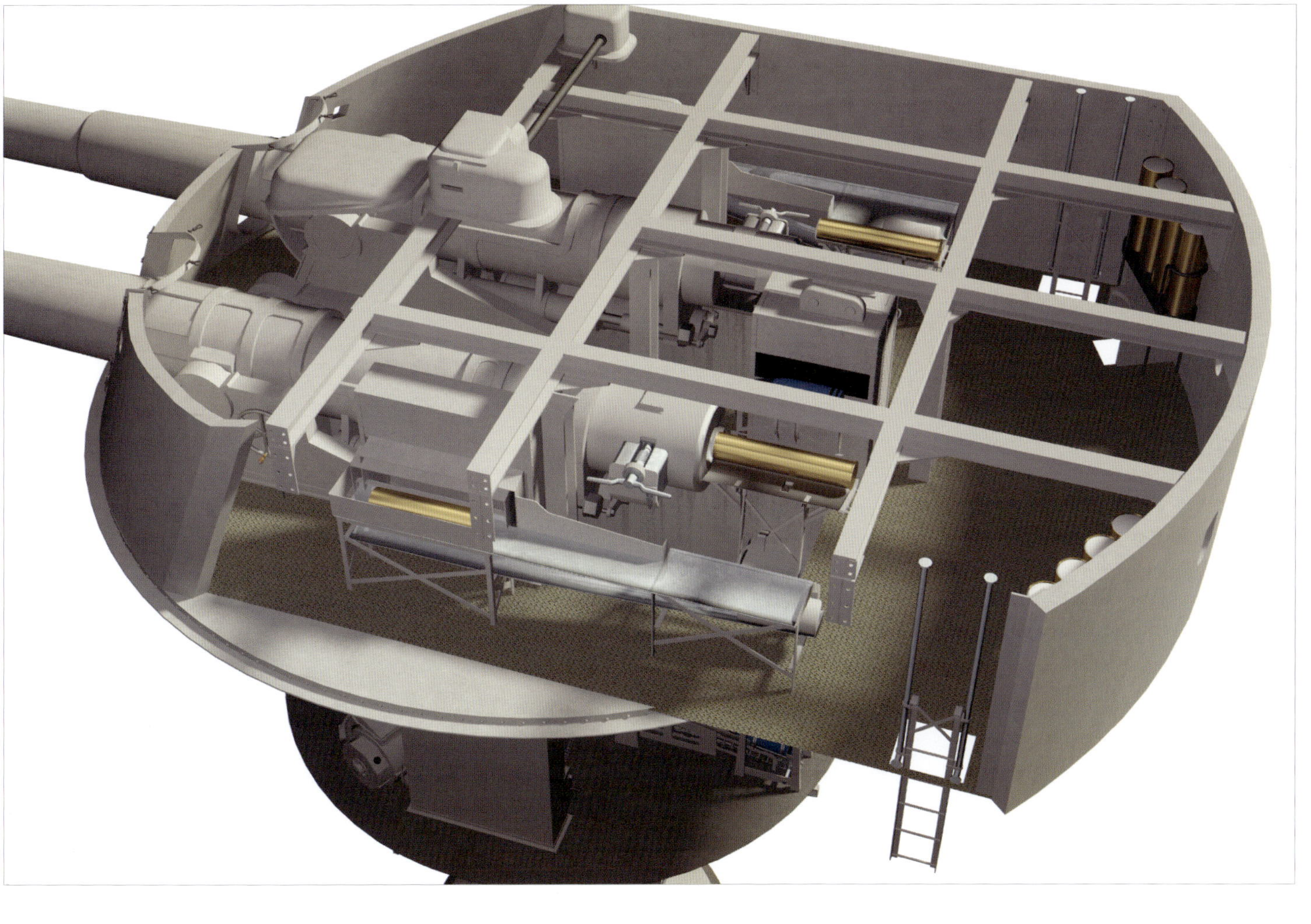

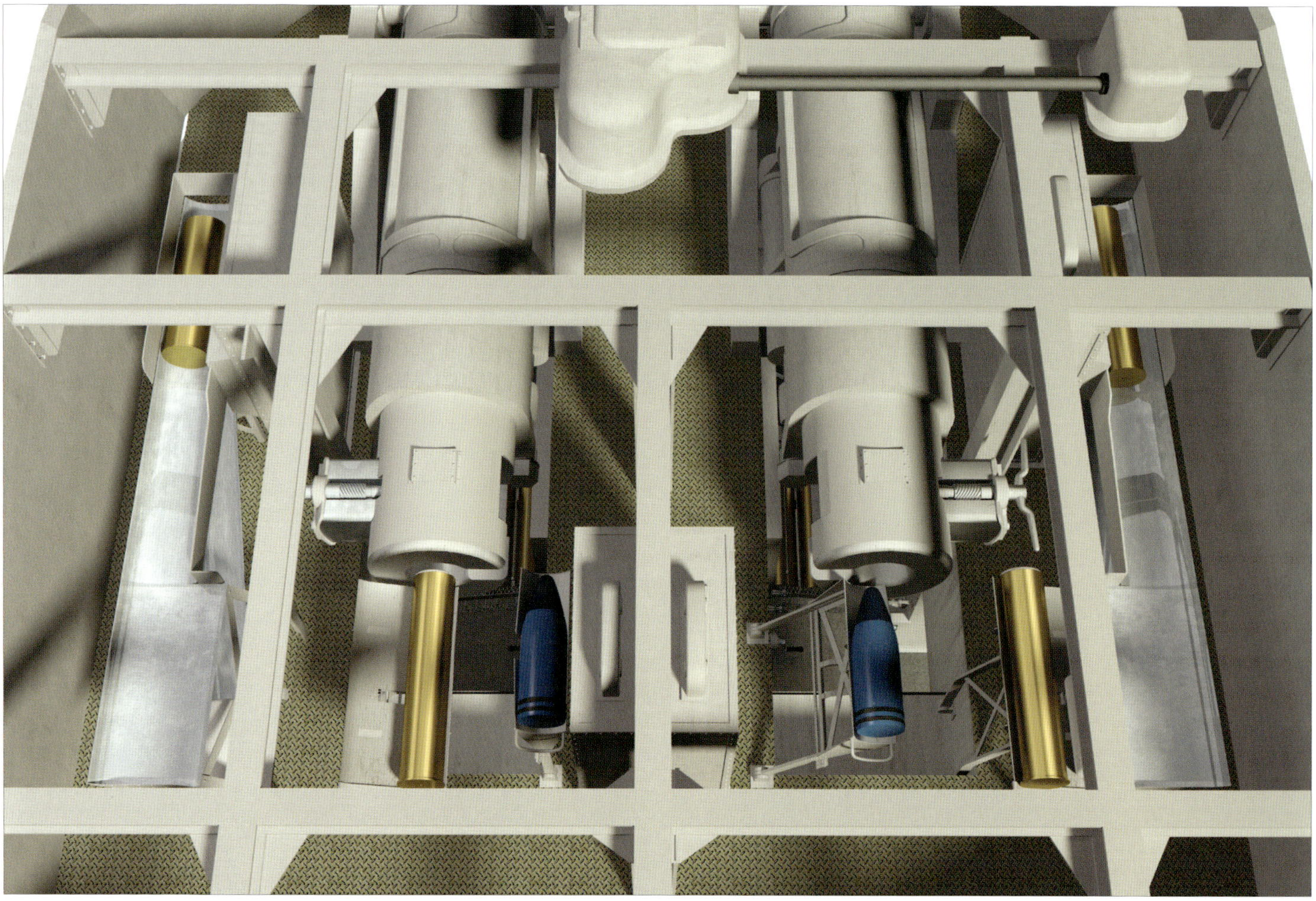

The propellant was ejected from the two lifts (left and right) onto a metal slide then pushed along to the breech for loading.

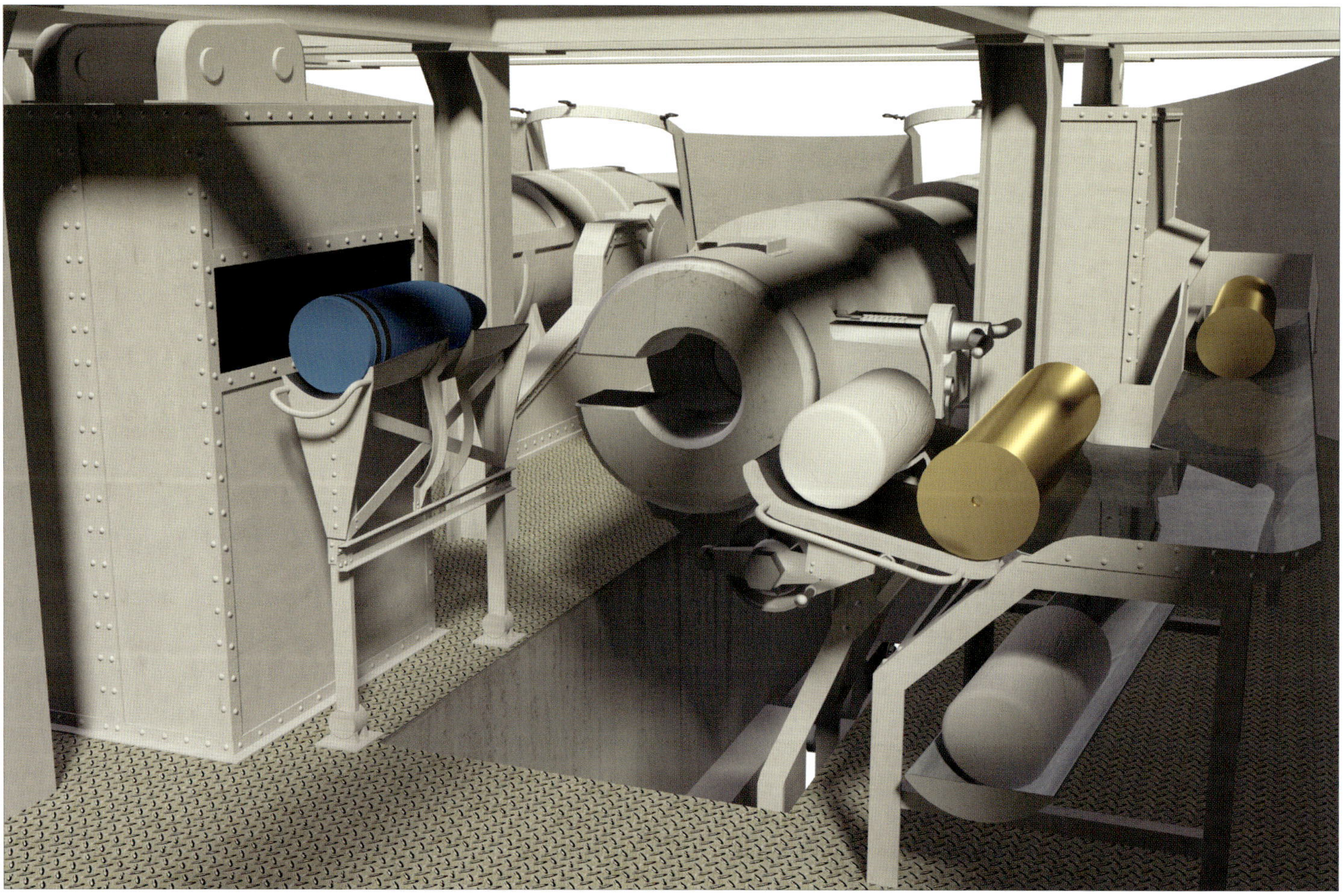

The transfer platform is where the ammunition would change lifts. The top electric motors (under the cogwheels) are for the turret rotation and the hand cranks for manual rotation in case of loss of electric power. On the platform are two electrically driven three cylinder hydraulic pumps which provide the power to elevate the guns. The lower platform has the electric motors for the ammunition lifts and the hand cranks for manual operating when power is lost.

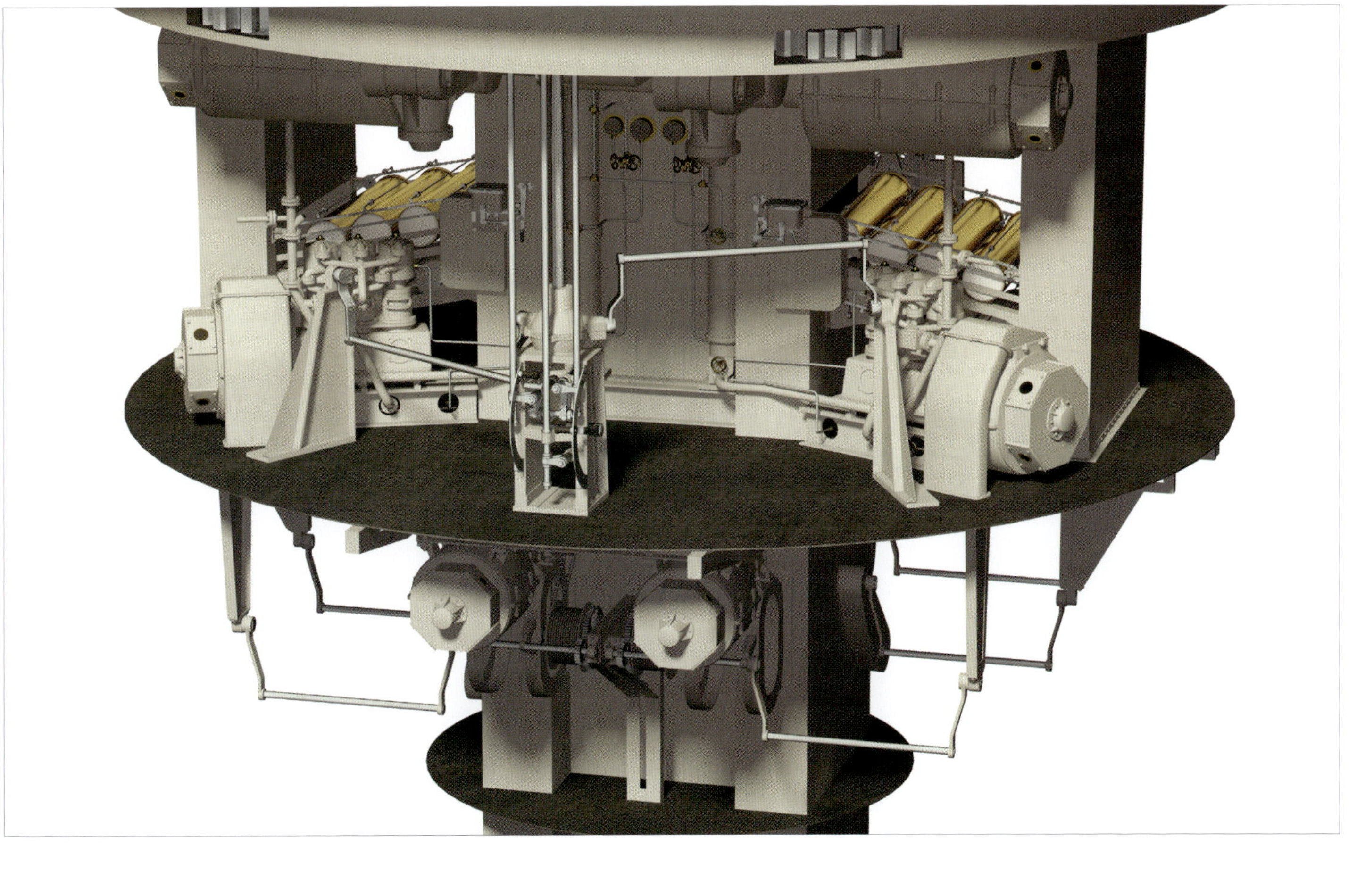

The propellant transfer mechanism. The casing above and the fore charge below.

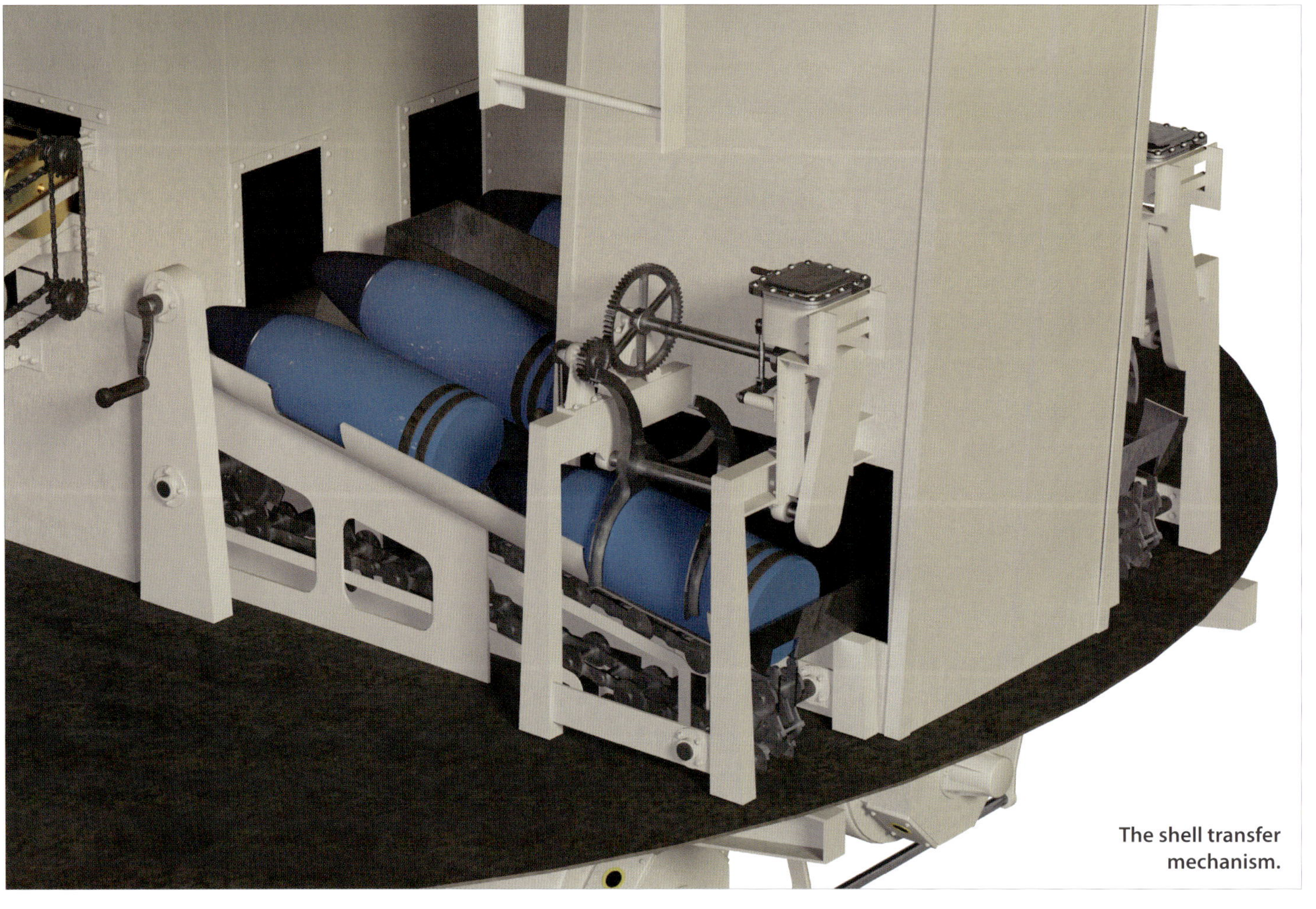

The shell transfer mechanism.

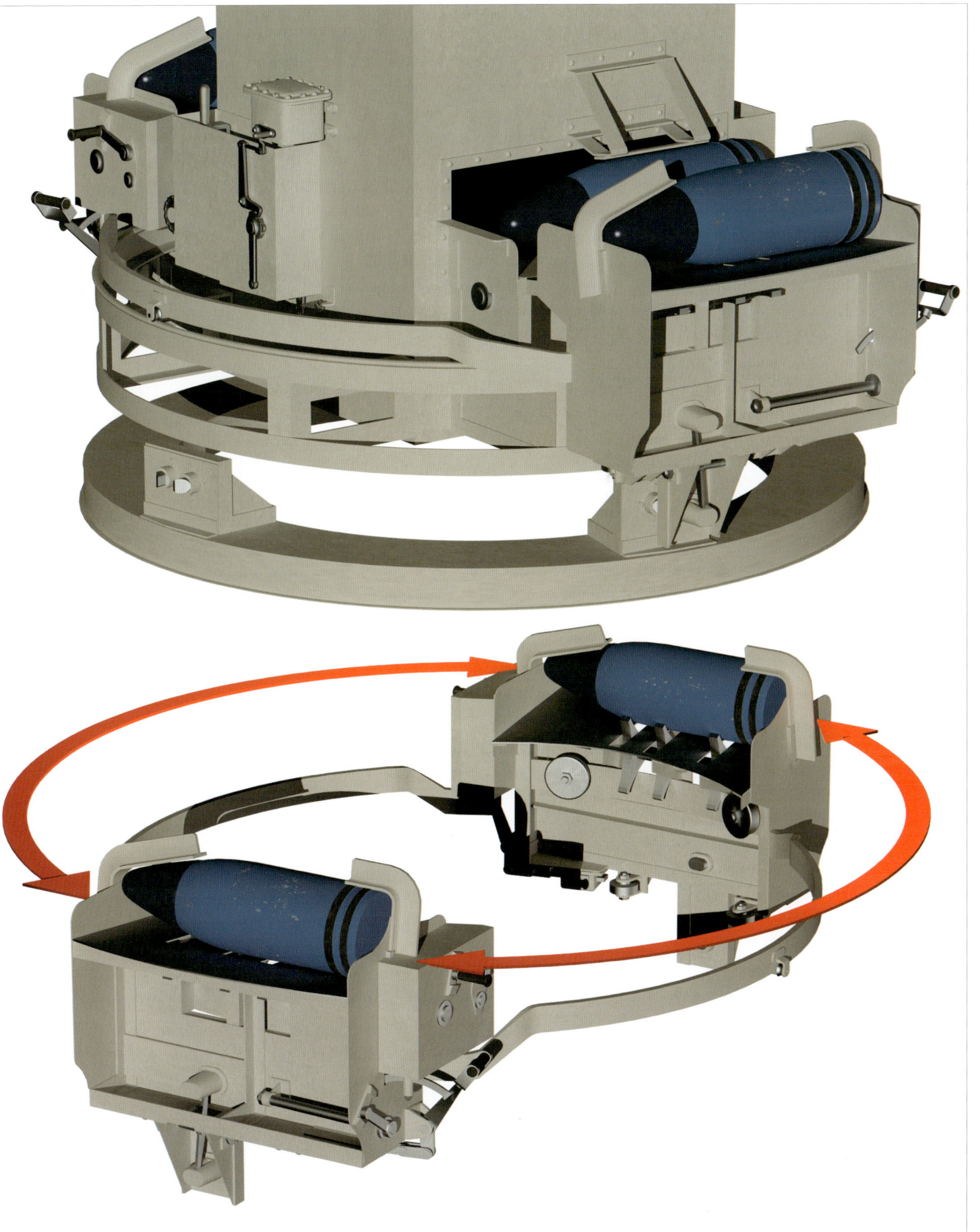

The shell loading mechanism. A rotating transfer carriage made the loading of the heavy projectiles easier.

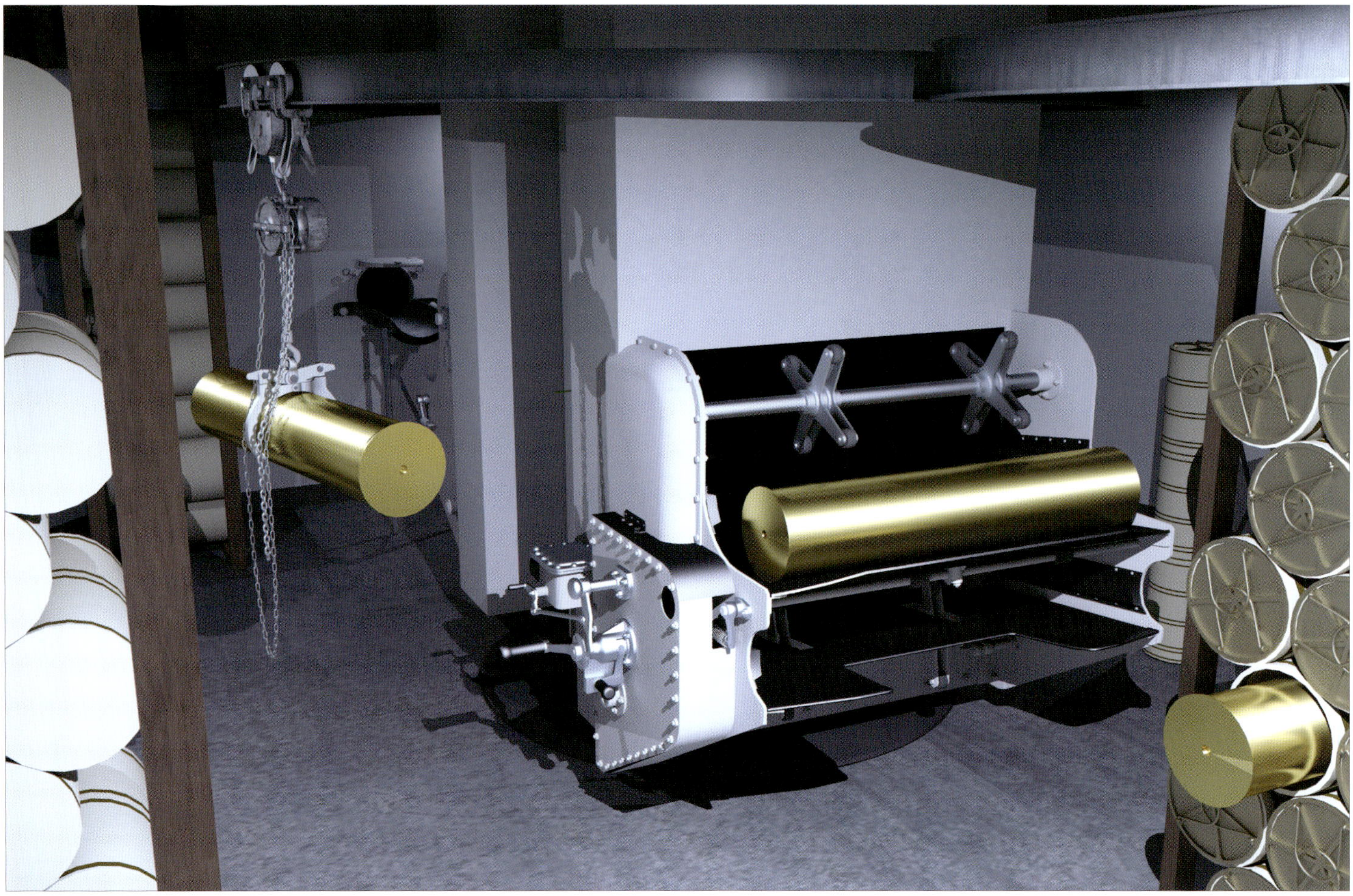

A view inside the powder magazine.

A view inside the projectile magazine.

15 cm /45 on a M.P.L. C/1906 mounting.

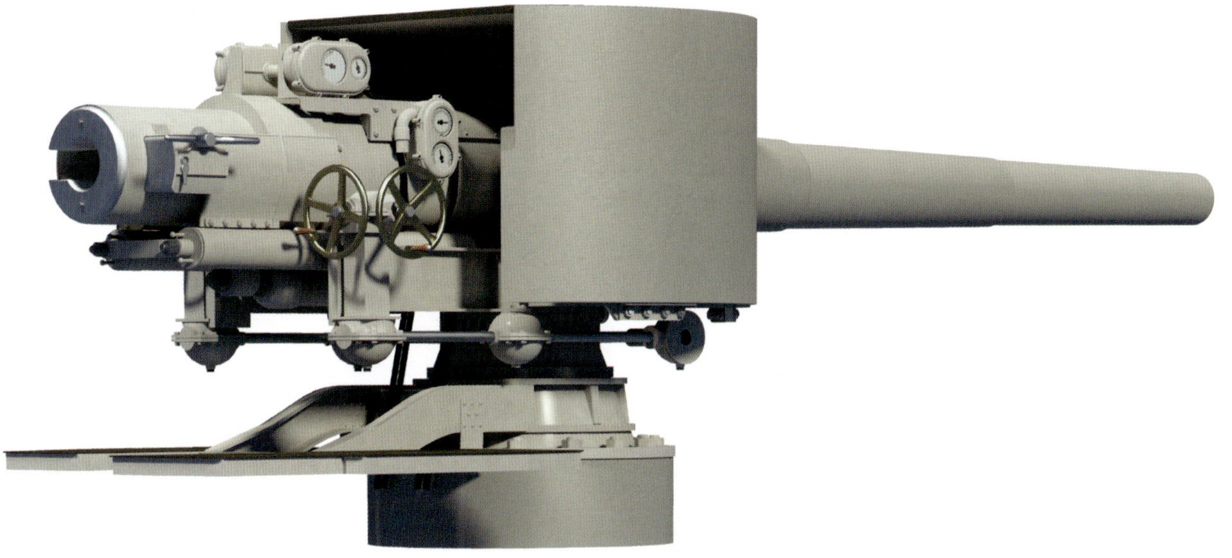

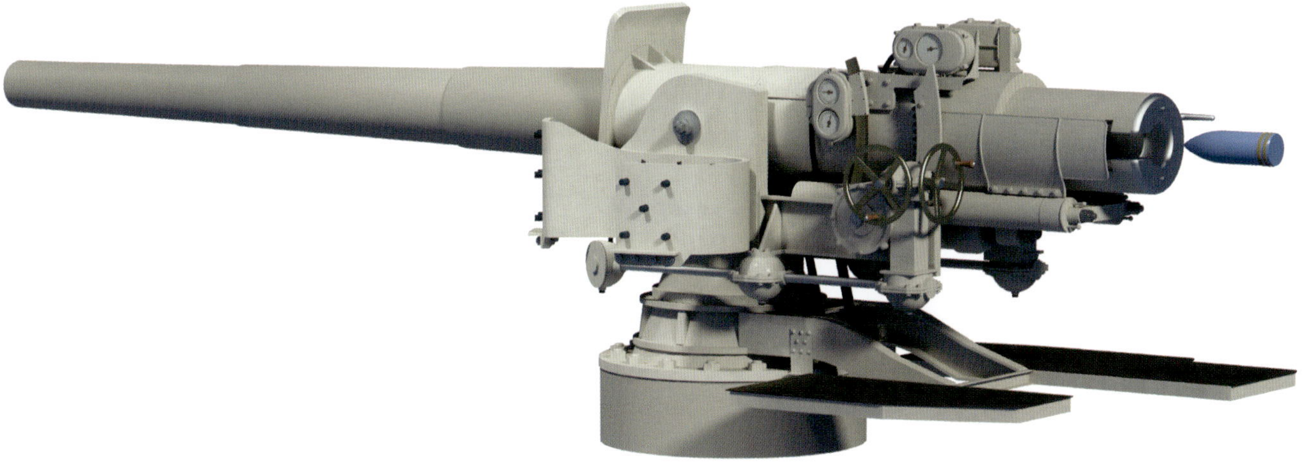

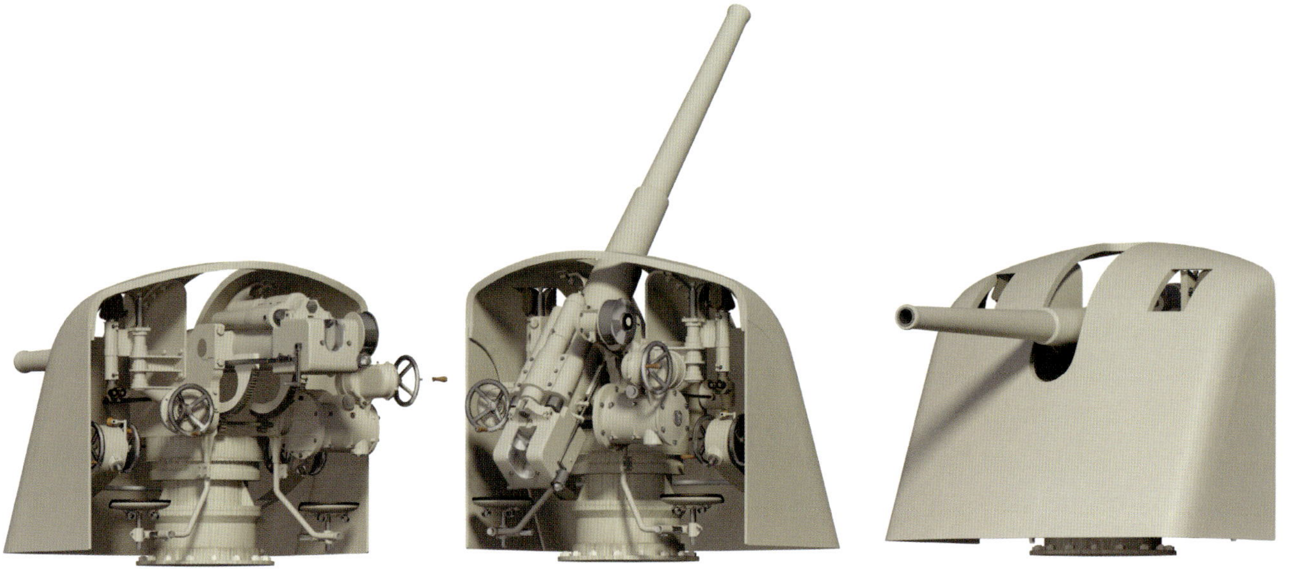

8.8cm/45 FLAK L/45.

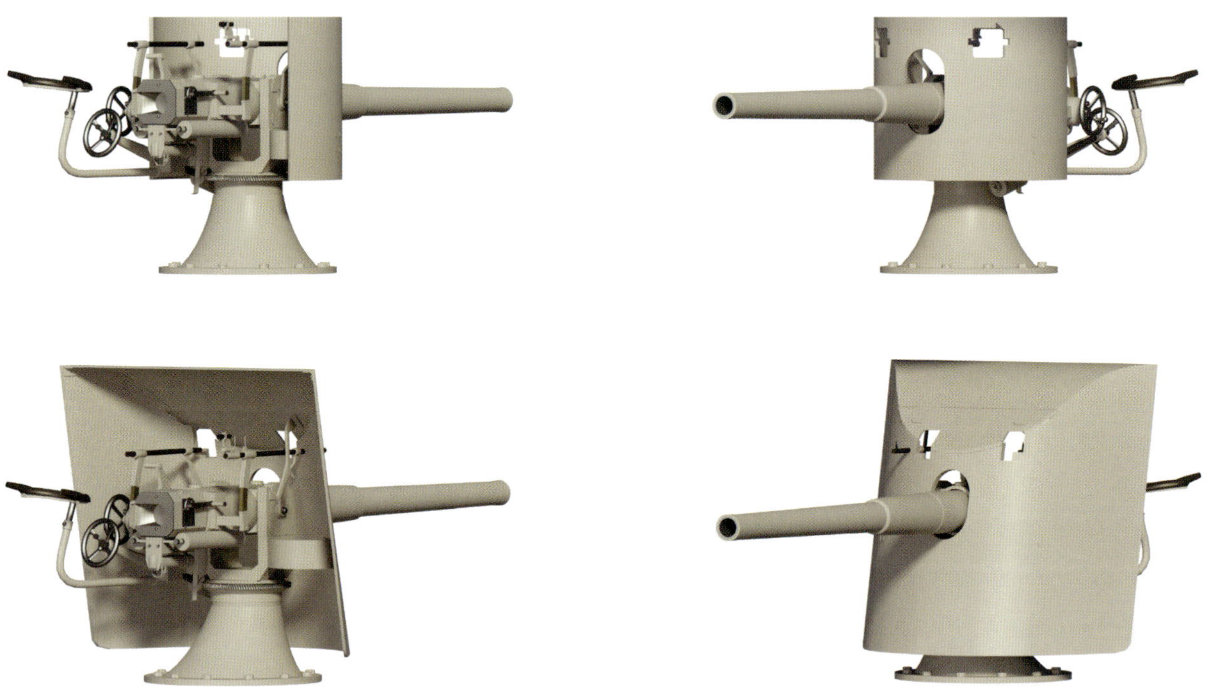

8.8 cm/45 SK L/45 in MPL C/06 Mounting.

110 cm naval searchlight.

MG 08 in a removable mounting.

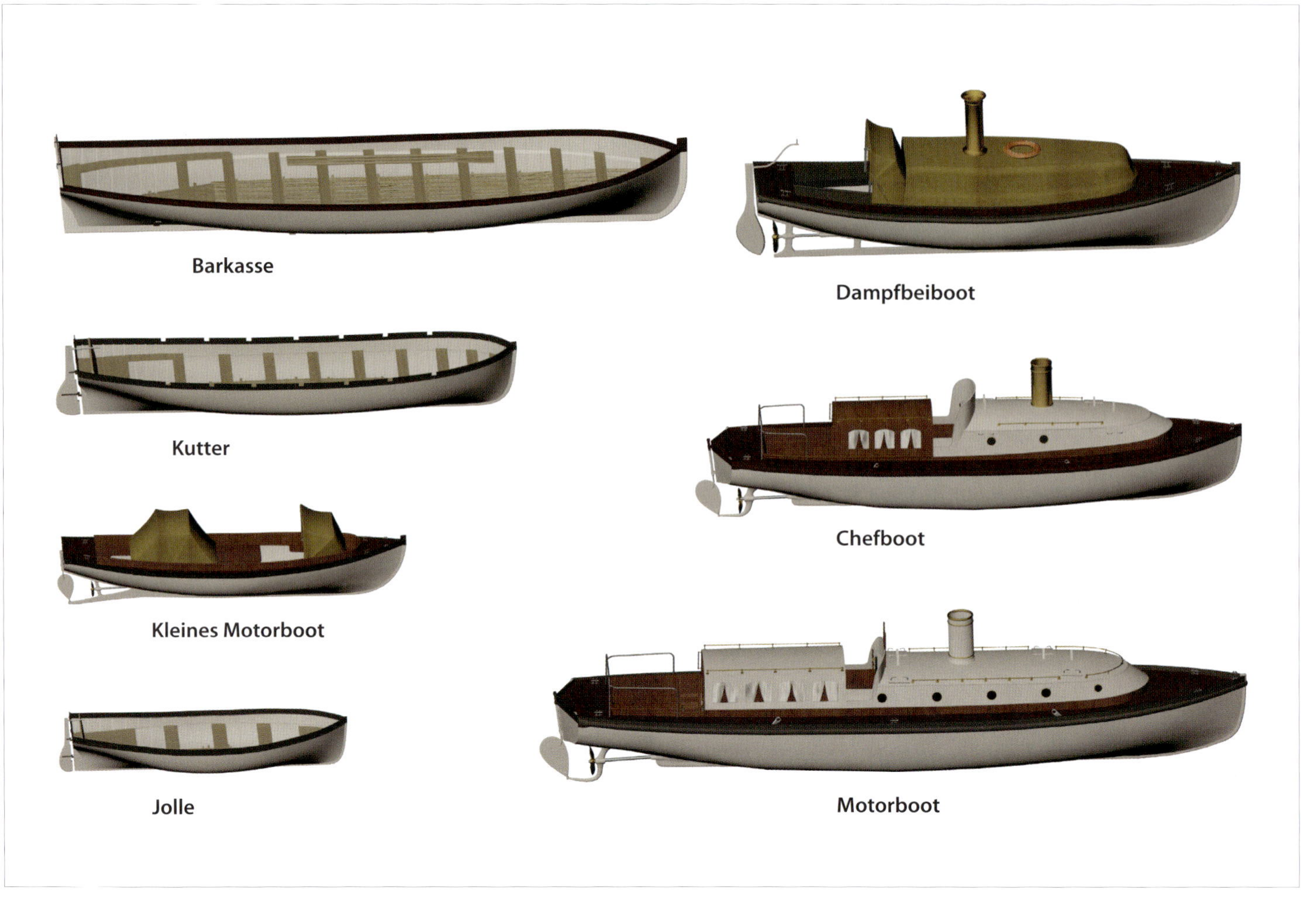
Barkasse
Dampfbeiboot
Kutter
Chefboot
Kleines Motorboot
Jolle
Motorboot

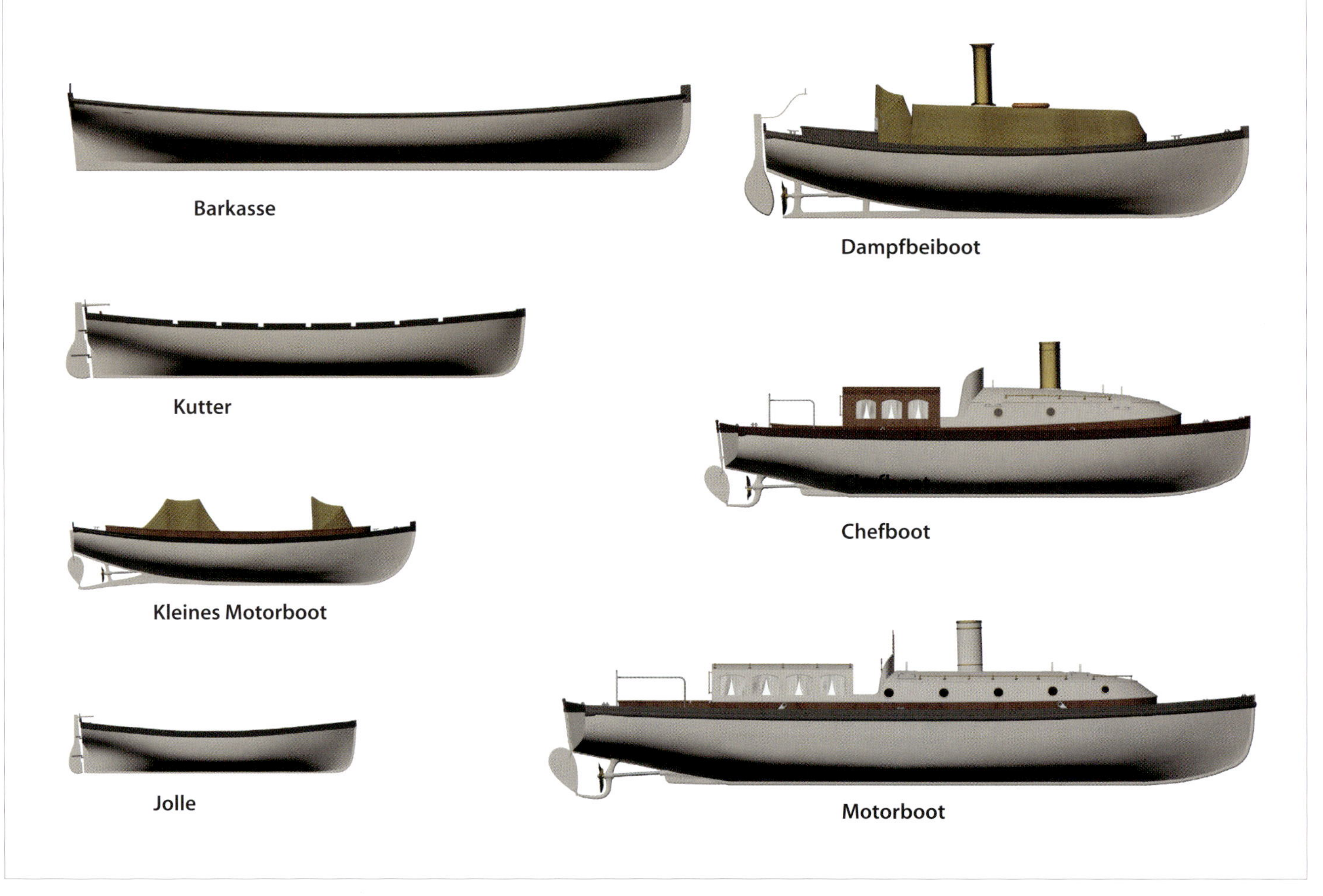
Barkasse
Dampfbeiboot
Kutter
Chefboot
Kleines Motorboot
Jolle
Motorboot

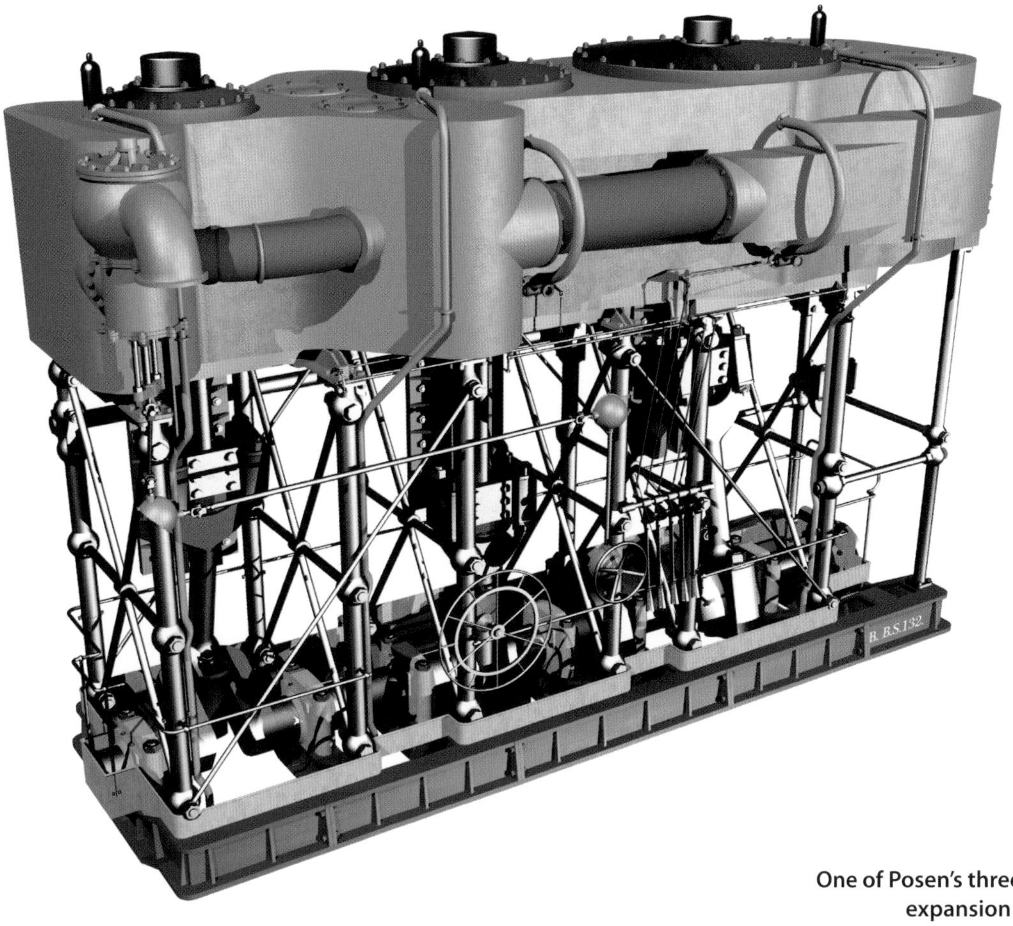

One of Posen's three cylinder triple expansion steam engines.

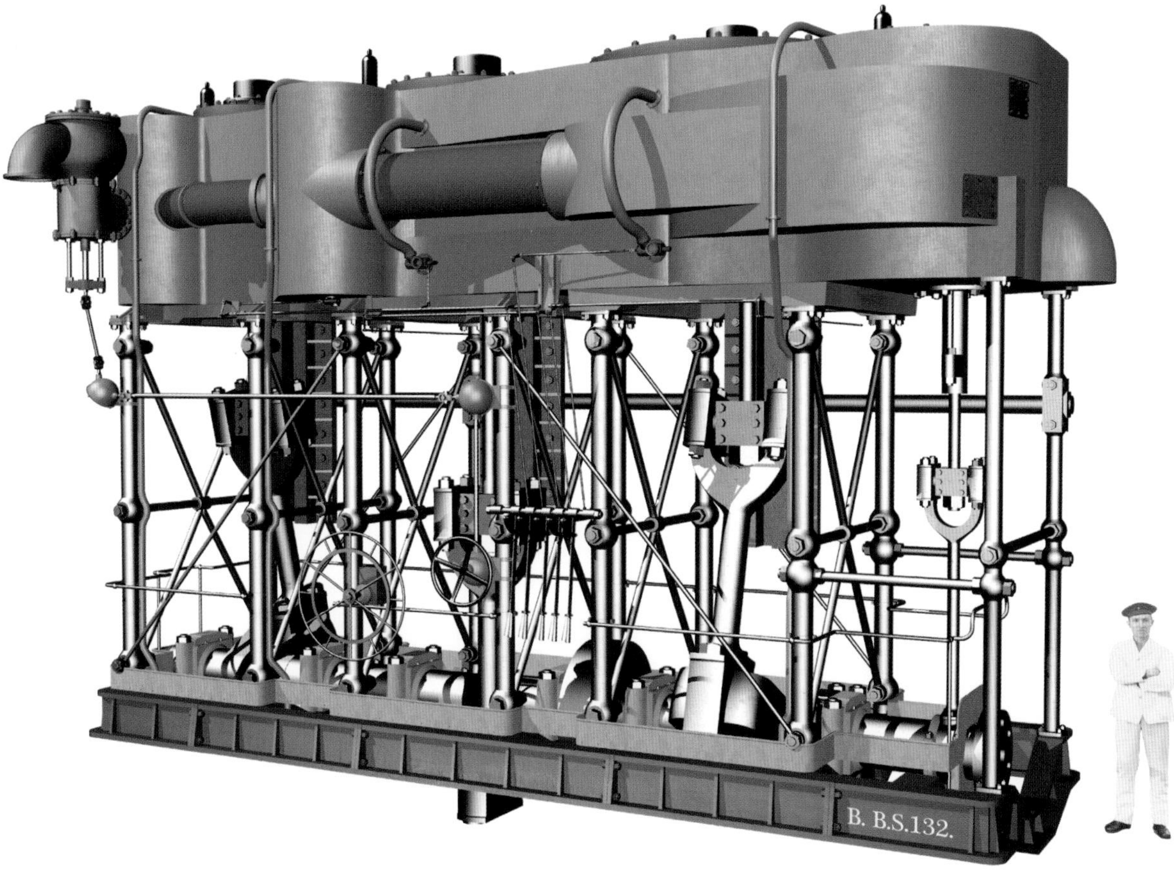

Most of the larger warships in the Kaiserliche Marine were fitted out to retrieve and launch aircraft during the war.

The FF33e Friedrichshafen was unable to fold its wings so finding a position on some warships was not simple. The FF33e's wingspan was 16.80 Meters.

The FF33e Friedrichshafen entered service in the summer of 1915. The aircraft used the Benz Bz III engine which gave a top speed of 123 km/h and a flight duration of 5 hours. The aircraft could carry three 10 kg or six 5 kg bombs, or if used for reconnaissance a radio transmitter was fitted.

Placing the aircraft on D turret's roof with the boat's crane.

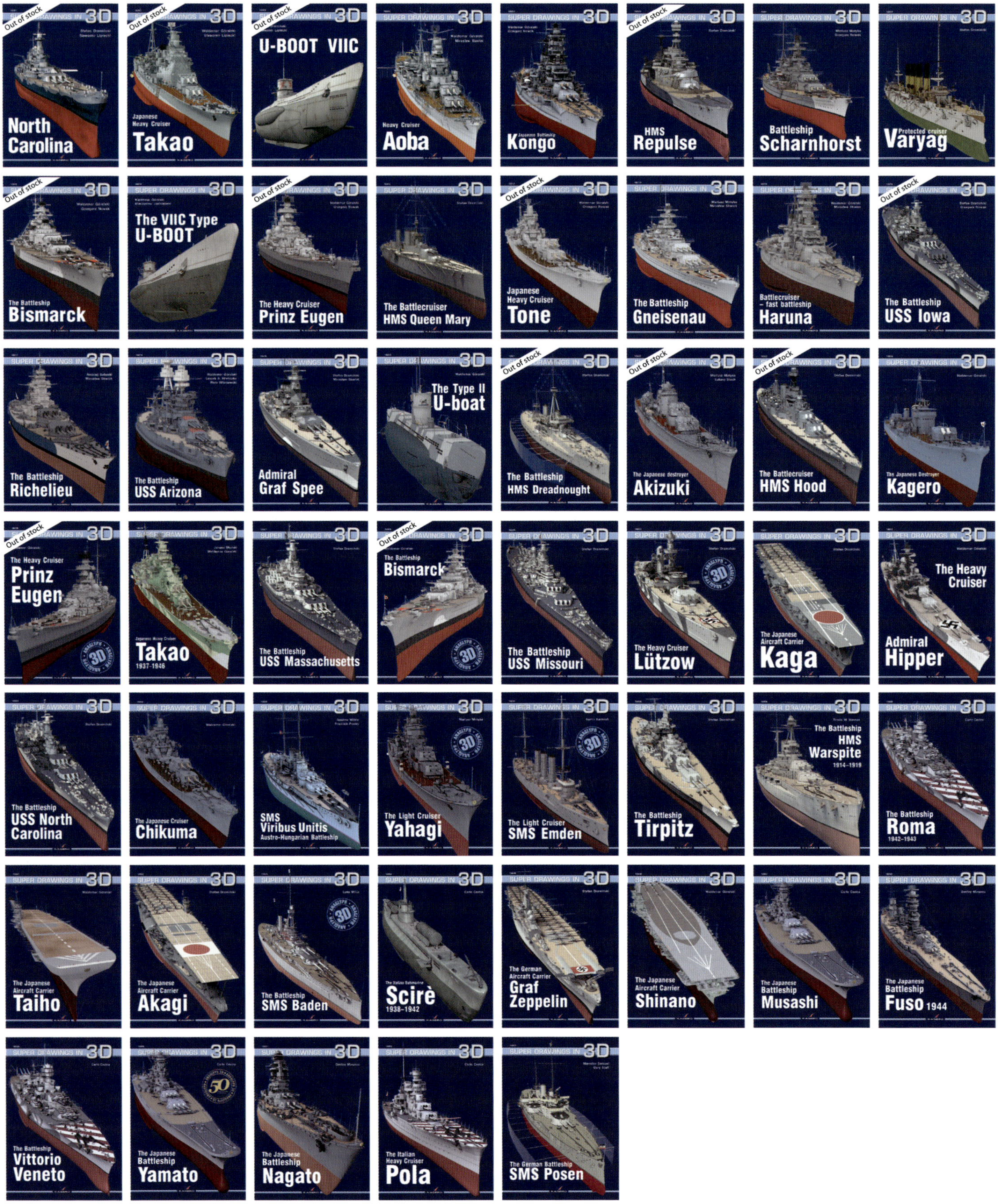

The German Battleship SMS Posen – Marsden Samuel, Gary Staff
LUBLIN 2017 • ISBN 978-83-65437-53-2

3D illustrations and captions, text: Marsden Samuel, Gary Staff • Proof-reading: Tomasz Basarabowicz • Design: KAGERO STUDIO – Marcin Wachowicz
KAGERO Publishing • www.kagero.pl, e-mail: kagero@kagero.pl, marketing@kagero.pl
Editorial office, Marketing, Distribution: KAGERO Publishing, Akacjowa 100, os. Borek, Turka, 20-258 Lublin 62, Poland, phone/fax (+48) 81 501 21 05
www.kagero.eu